A PRACTICAL GUIDE TO
CARING FOR
YOUR HORSE

A PRACTICAL GUIDE TO
CARING FOR YOUR HORSE

*A comprehensive handbook for successful
horse and pony care: buying a horse,
stable management, equipment,
grooming and basic first aid*

JUDITH DRAPER

Photography by Kit Houghton

LORENZ BOOKS

This edition is published by Lorenz Books
an imprint of Anness Publishing Ltd
Blaby Road, Wigston, Leicestershire LE18 4SE
info@anness.com

www.lorenzbooks.com; www.annesspublishing.com

If you like the images in this book and would like to investigate using them for publishing, promotions
or advertising, please visit our website www.practicalpictures.com for more information.

© Anness Publishing Ltd 2013

A CIP catalogue record for this book is available from the British Library.

Publisher: Joanna Lorenz
Senior Editor: Clare Nicholson
Project Editor: Marion Paull
Designer: Michael Morey
Illustrator: Rodney Paull
Production Controller: Pirong Wang

PUBLISHER'S NOTE
Although the advice and information in this book are believed to be accurate and true at the
time of going to press, neither the authors nor the publisher can accept any legal responsibility
or liability for any errors or omissions that may have been made nor for any inaccuracies nor for
any loss, harm or injury that comes about from following instructions or advice in this book.

Contents

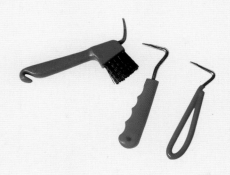

Horse and Pony Care

Buying a Horse

Everyone who takes part in sport on a regular basis reaches the stage when they want their own equipment. Whether it is a tennis racquet, a fencing foil, a pair of skis or a yacht, owning rather than hiring makes life easier on two counts: the equipment will be available whenever it is required and, most importantly, the owner's performance will almost certainly improve because that equipment will have been selected with their skills and limitations in mind. Riders, however, are faced with a problem not encountered by other sportsmen: their most important piece of equipment is not a man-made object which, to varying degrees, can be tailored to fit individual needs.

The horse is a living creature, with a mind, will and personality of his own. He is an expensive animal both to buy and to keep. Choosing the right one is not always easy; choosing the wrong one can be disastrous, both for an owner's bank balance and for his or her confidence. The prospective horse owner should proceed with caution and the rewards will be great.

Choosing the Right Horse

Before you buy a horse make an honest assessment of your riding ability, bearing in mind that most people tend to over-estimate their skill. Talented, experienced riders get the best from all sorts of horses, even those with difficult temperaments. They can school and bring on the young horse, improve the poorly educated older one and ensure that the well-trained performer is used to the best effect. A novice rider, who has only just mastered the basics of horsemanship, can do none of these things and should choose a mount accordingly. The novice needs a correctly schooled, well-mannered mount with a kind disposition, one who will look after his rider. The term "schoolmaster" is aptly used to describe these equine paragons.

For the majority of people cost is one of the most important factors and the purchase price will be determined by a number of things: the type, size and conformation of the horse or pony; its age; its temperament and manners; its performance capabilities (either proven or potential) and its

■ **PREVIOUS PAGE OPPOSITE**
A Dartmoor pony: a suitable ride for a child.

■ **PREVIOUS PAGE**
A Karbardin horse: ideal for endurance riding.

■ **LEFT**
With the right horse, the experience of ownership will be enjoyable and rewarding for both horse and rider.

■ **RIGHT**
The majority of warmbloods, specifically developed as sports horses, make fine show jumpers. This horse is a Holstein.

■ **BELOW**
The larger British native ponies, like this Highland, are suitable for adult riders as well as children. They are economical to keep.

level of schooling. Generally speaking, an unbroken two- or three-year-old will be cheaper than a four- or five-year-old which has already received some schooling; after that the horse gradually increases in value until it reaches the age of about ten. Once into its teens, it will tend to decrease in value.

Apart from price, your choice of horse or pony will be determined by your size and weight; your riding ability; your stabling/grazing facilities;

the amount of time you have to look after it, and the use to which you intend to put it. For example, there is no point in spending a lot of money on a flighty Thoroughbred if you are a nervous rider who wants to do no more than go for quiet hacks; similarly, a pure-bred Arab is not going to take you to the top in the show-jumping world. As to size, much depends on your own build – someone with long legs will certainly be more comfortable on a big horse than someone with short legs and vice versa, and it is usually easier to ride well if you are neither under- nor over-horsed. Temperament and manners are a vital consideration, too. Nervous riders need placid (though not lazy) mounts if they are not to be frightened and put off riding altogether, while a bolder rider will be able to cope with, and enjoy, a more spirited ride.

■ **BELOW**
If quiet hacks out are your aim, make sure you don't choose the horse who is too spirited.

■ **RIGHT**
For endurance riding, choose a horse with proven stamina. Arabs and part-bred Arabs are particularly suited to the higher levels of this sport.

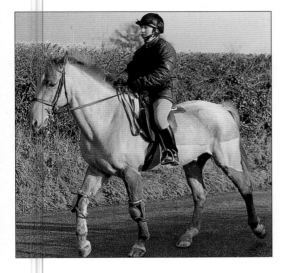

■ **BELOW**
If quiet hacks out are your aim, make sure you don't choose the horse who is too spirited.

■ **BOTTOM**
Experienced riders will be able to school young horses, but novice riders should learn on a more experienced horse.

Then there is the question of how much time you can devote to looking after your horse. If you have a full-time job, and limited time for weekday exercising, life will be easier for you and your horse if he can live out or at least be turned out during the day.

If you are not planning to do a lot of strenuous competition work, then age need not be too much of a factor, though of course the older the animal the more work he is likely to have done and the more wear and tear there will have been on his legs and body by the time you buy him. However, for general riding purposes horses and ponies often go on well into their late teens and even early twenties. A young horse will, of course, have many more useful years ahead of him and will be easier to sell on for a good price. However, young horses are not suitable for the novice rider, who will be unable to give them the necessary schooling.

Unless you are planning to become involved in an activity which requires a specific breed – such as a particular category of showing – you will have a wide variety of breeds and types to choose from. Always bear in mind, however, your intended use for the horse: for endurance riding he will need great stamina; for eventing, stamina plus speed; for dressage, excellent movement. While stallions often excel in the last named discipline and are increasingly seen in other types of equine competition as well, they do require more expert handling than geldings and mares, and are not suitable for the novice horse owner. Mares can be more moody and take rather more understanding than geldings (very often, though, a good competition mare is very good indeed). They do, of course, come into season regularly during the summer months and this can be a problem.

If you have good stabling and grazing facilities, you can keep any type or breed without a problem. Lack of stabling will tend to determine what you can or cannot buy, particularly if you live in a region where the winters are cold and wet and/or the summers excessively hot. A British native pony

will do perfectly well living out all year round, provided supplementary feed is given in winter, as necessary. A thin-skinned Thoroughbred, on the other hand, may not thrive unless he has the shelter of a stable, at least at night. If you wish to keep your horse at peak fitness for competition work or hunting, you will certainly need the use of a stable.

Where to Buy

There are various ways to buy a horse. These include at a public sale, through a dealer, from a private vendor advertising in the equestrian or local press, or perhaps from the riding school where you have been taking lessons.

The novice rider is generally advised not to buy at a public sale. The problem is not that all sales are conducted by less than reputable people – that is certainly not the case – but that everything takes place so quickly and there may not be sufficient opportunity for the purchaser to ride the horse. Buying in this way calls for an expert, practised eye and it is incumbent upon the purchaser to be observant. For instance, if a horse offered for sale has an obvious physical defect, the onus is on the purchaser to see it – a subsequent plea of ignorance will not be accepted. On the other hand the horse must correspond to its description – a horse described as a show jumper must be able to jump – and the buyer is entitled to return it if this proves not to be the case (or, if necessary, to sue for damages).

Dealers are businessmen with a reputation to maintain and are unlikely to try to sell you a bad lot. Your local riding school may be able to put you in touch with one or, failing that, you may see them advertising in the equestrian press. The advantages of buying through a dealer are that you will almost certainly have the choice of several horses and there should be plenty of opportunity to see them being handled and to ride them yourself. Some dealers may also allow you to try the horse at home and, if you have a horse to sell, may offer part-exchange terms.

Buying from a private vendor – and there are always a great many advertising in the equestrian and farming press as well as in local newspapers – may seem the simplest way of acquiring a horse but it is not necessarily the safest. Here the rule is *caveat emptor* (let the buyer beware), a common law maxim warning you that you cannot claim that your purchase is defective if you have not obtained express guarantees from the vendor. Many of the horses and ponies described in the "For Sale" columns are up for sale for perfectly genuine reasons but others may not be. It is easy to compose an advertisement praising their good points but omitting their shortcomings. Just because a horse is good to box and shoe does not mean that he is quiet to clip or sensible in traffic. The brilliant jumper may refuse to go into a horsebox or trailer. The otherwise perfect equine specimen may, when you get him home, persist in jumping out of his paddock, refuse to be caught, or chew his stable, his rugs, his bandages – or all three. Often it is not so much what the advertisement does say but what it omits to say, so you must be prepared to ask the right questions.

If you have been attending a good riding school, the proprietor should be able to advise on the purchase of a horse or pony and may well have one on the premises which would suit you. The advantage here is that the instructor will have a good knowledge of your skills and limitations as a rider.

Trying a Horse

■ BELOW
When trying a horse, ride him at different paces and have a jump if you wish.

When you learn of a horse which you think may suit your purpose, the first step is to make an appointment to see it and try it. Always take a more knowledgeable person along with you both to offer expert advice and to act as a witness to any sale. If you have no one who will do this as a friend, it is worth paying for an expert opinion.

Explain to the vendor exactly what you want to use the horse for and ask specific questions: is the horse good to box, clip, shoe, catch, in traffic, etc. Ask to see the horse led up outside and pay close attention to how he behaves while he is having his rugs removed and his bridle put on. Note the bit which is being used. Cast an eye around the inside of the stable and the door for signs of kick marks or chewing. It may be that this is not the horse's usual box but if it is, such signs could indicate a behavioural problem. Ask to see the horse stood up outside and view him from both sides to assess his conformation before having him walked and trotted up. Make sure that he is trotted up on a loose rein both away from you and towards you (leading a horse on a short rein can help to cover up defective action).

Before you ride him, watch the vendor put him through his paces to see how he goes with a familiar rider. Then ask your expert adviser to try him. If the vendor failed to ask the horse to do certain things, such as strike off on a particular leg at canter, it may be that there is a problem, and your adviser (who should have noticed even if you have not) can look into the matter. Finally, ride the horse yourself. Does he feel right for you: not too big, not too wide, not too narrow? Is there a good length of rein? Put him through his paces, have a jump if you wish, take him out on the road to make sure he is safe in traffic and generally try to get the feel of him.

It is not easy in a relatively short time to assess whether this is the horse you really want to have on a long-term basis, so if possible arrange to have him at home on trial, say for a week. This will enable you to get to know his character, to ride him in more relaxed circumstances and also to get to know more about his general behaviour: is he well mannered in the stable, is he good in the company of other horses, will he willingly go away from other horses, is he safe in the company of dogs and in all traffic (not just cars) and so on. However well he suits you from the riding point of view, it is important that you should actually like him, too.

If you do decide to have a horse on trial, make sure that the arrangements are agreed and set down in writing – you will be responsible for feed, vet's bills and so on and will be liable for negligence.

Horses sold at public sales usually come with a warranty or warranties. A warranty is a statement of fact made before or during a transaction – for example a horse may be "warranted sound". Privately sold horses do not always come with a warranty and if you ask the vendor for one and he or she declines, then you may have grounds for suspicion (on the other hand, in these days of increasing litigation, the vendor may simply be being extra cautious). When in doubt, consult your expert equestrian adviser and, if necessary, a solicitor. The law does give some protection to buyers of horses, as in the case of other merchandise, the big difference being that the horse is a living creature and therefore far less predictable than, say, a television or a refrigerator or a motor car.

When you do find the horse of your dreams and decide to purchase, buy him "subject to a veterinary certificate" and ask your own veterinary surgeon (not the vendor's) to carry out the inspection.

Vetting

If possible, you should be present when your veterinary surgeon carries out his examination of your proposed purchase so that he can discuss the horse with you.

The examination will begin with a preliminary visual inspection. The vet can deduce a good deal from the general attitude of the horse when approached: his stance might show signs of lameness; the condition of his stable could indicate behavioural problems such as box-walking (constant pacing round and round the stable), assuming that the vendor has not switched the horse to another box to hide the evidence; his head carriage can indicate problems of balance or vision; how he reacts to being handled will be indicative of his temperament.

The vet will take in the horse's general state of health, noting any discharges from the nose or eyes, the condition of the skin; and the

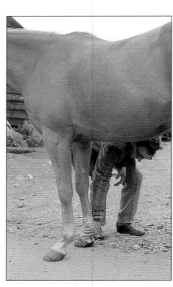

presence of lesions, or heat in a tendon or joint. He will also examine the eyes and heart.

Once outside his stable, the horse will be stood up squarely on flat ground while the vet makes a detailed appraisal of his conformation. This is followed by a manual examination of

the entire horse: the head, including the mouth and teeth, the neck, ribs, sternum, back, abdomen and the limbs. Once the horse has been examined at rest he will be walked and then trotted in hand both away from the vet and towards him to enable him to detect any signs of lameness. Turning the horse to either side on a tight circle, backing him for a few strides and lungeing him at trot on a hard, flat surface are other tests which may reveal problems of unsoundness.

Flexion tests may be carried out on the limbs, particularly if there is a suspicion of lameness. However, opinion differs on these flexion tests, as they can actually induce lameness if they are used with sufficient force.

■ **ABOVE LEFT**
Vetting includes a manual examination of the entire horse.

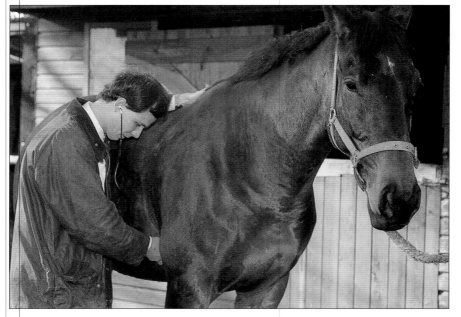

■ **LEFT**
The vet will check the horse's heart and respiratory rates both at rest and after exercise.

▌ LEFT
The horse stands
outside the stable
while a detailed
appraisal is made
of his conformation.

▌ BELOW
During the vetting
procedure the horse
will be warmed up
under saddle, then
given a gallop. Fast
work sometimes
produces signs of
an old lameness
problem.

To test the horse's wind and heart he is tacked up, warmed up gently at walk, trot and canter and then given a gallop. The vet will note whether the horse dips its back when the saddle is put on and the rider mounts. Some horses habitually do this, in others it may be a sign of back problems. After exercise the vet will listen to the lungs for any signs of abnormal respiration and to the heart for any irregularity. After the horse has been cooled off he will be rested for half an hour, after which he will be trotted out again in hand. If the horse is suffering from muscular or arthritic problems, which might disappear while the horse is warm, they may well reappear after this period of rest. Signs of old lameness might also appear after fast exercise. A further examination of the heart and respiration may also be made. The vet will then complete the certificate.

The certificate includes a detailed identification of the horse, the vet's report and his opinion as to its suitability for purchase, bearing in mind the use for which it is required. It is important to remember that the certificate is not a guarantee, but an opinion expressed by a qualified person. The certificate means that the horse has been found to be free of certain disorders at the time of examination. It does not and cannot mean that the horse is and will remain completely free from disease – vets are certainly not clairvoyant. Nor does the certificate guarantee that the horse is free from so-called stable "vices" such as crib-biting or weaving. If you would like a written warranty to this effect, you must obtain it from the vendor.

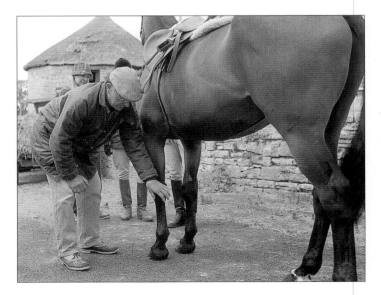

Keeping a Horse

Horse ownership is a big responsibility and should not be entered into lightly. Certainly no one should consider it unless they have the necessary facilities and have first mastered the rudiments of horse care. These include a knowledge of feeding, grooming, general stable management and basic first aid. All horses and ponies need safe accommodation and daily attention – they cannot be set aside on a Sunday afternoon and forgotten about until the following weekend. Unlike small domesticated animals, who share their owners' home, they need large facilities of their own, maintenance of which takes time and money. Depending on the work required of them and their breed or type, horses can either be kept at grass or stabled, or a combination of the two (known as the combined system). The owner will therefore need access to grazing, a stable, a weatherproof storage area for feed, bedding and tools and somewhere secure to keep tack and other equipment.

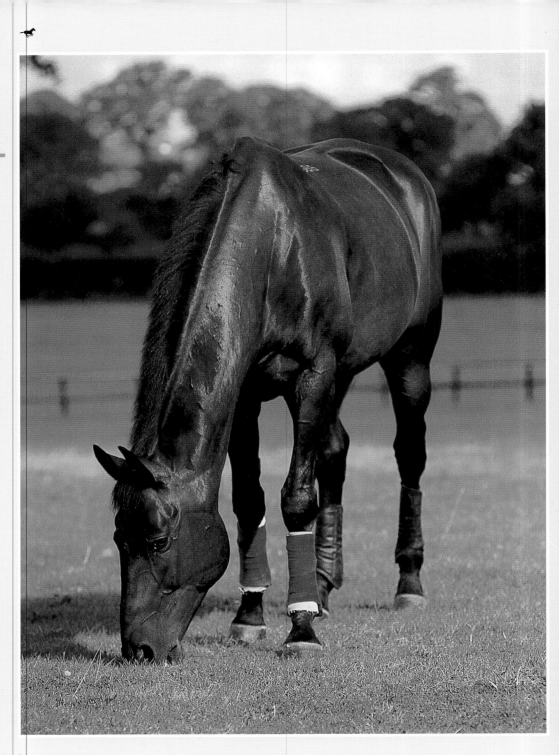

THE HORSE AT GRASS

The horse is by nature a nomadic, grazing animal, so it is far more natural – and less stressful – to keep him in a paddock than in a stable. However, a fenced paddock, no matter how large, is still an unnatural environment for a horse and certain precautions must be taken if the horse is to be safe and secure.

▌ PREVIOUS PAGE OPPOSITE Stabled horses need
constant care and attention.
▌ PREVIOUS PAGE Most small ponies are quite hardy and
can live outside all year round.
▌ OPPOSITE Fit horses who spend part of the day at grass
should wear bandages and boots to guard against injury.
▌ ABOVE Brood mares grazing in a well-fenced paddock.

Fencing

All fields used for grazing horses must be securely and safely fenced. Since it is the horse's nature to roam, if he sees a gap he will certainly go for it. Similarly, if there is anything on which the horse can injure himself, he will find it – the domesticated horse is notoriously accident prone.

Undoubtedly the most effective (but unfortunately also the most expensive) fencing is good **wooden post and rail**. It is sturdy, long lasting and looks attractive. The wooden support posts, which should be 4 inches (10cm) square, must be driven well into the ground since horses like to rub against fencing, particularly when they are changing their coats. For a 4 foot (1.2m) fence the posts should be no less than 6 feet 6 inches (2m) in length. The fence should be constructed of good-quality wood and treated with non-toxic preservative to give protection against the weather and to discourage horses from chewing it. The top rail should be level with the top of the posts, which should be cut on a slope to allow rain to run off. Where possible the rails should be attached to the inner side of the posts. This prevents

▮ LEFT
Provided they are sufficiently high to deter the horse from jumping out, well-maintained stone walls are effective barriers.

▮ BELOW LEFT
Fixing the rails to the insides of the support posts prevents horses pushing them off when rubbing against them.

SAFETY CHECKLIST

- ☛ Make regular checks of all field boundaries.
- ☛ Repair any broken sections of boundary immediately.
- ☛ Keep wire fencing taut at all times.
- ☛ Set the lowest strand of a wire fence 18 inches (46cm) above the ground.
- ☛ Block off gaps in hedges with stout fencing – never use loose strands of wire.
- ☛ Never use pig or sheep netting – horses tend to put their feet through the squares of wire and can become caught up.
- ☛ Never use sheep posts, with sharp, upward pointing ends.
- ☛ Fence off potential danger areas, such as treacherous ground or ditches.
- ☛ When using electric fencing, ensure that it is visible – to humans as well as horses – by tying strips of strong plastic (for example, from feed or fertilizer bags) at intervals along the wire.
- ☛ Avoid metal or concrete fence posts – they will do far more damage than wooden ones should a horse collide with them.

Electric fencing has its uses, especially for temporarily dividing one area of a field from another, for example when resting one section of grazing.

Stone walls will also contain horses very well, provided they are sturdy and high enough – all boundaries should be a minimum of 4 feet (1.2m) high, otherwise horses might try to jump out. Like a hedge, a wall will afford some protection against the weather.

Modern **plastic fencing**, which comes in a variety of colours, may not look as "natural" as wood but it does have certain advantages: horses do not chew it, it does not rot and it will absorb impact without causing injury. Like wire, it should be correctly strained on strong, wooden posts.

Whatever the fencing used, right-angled or sharp corners should be avoided in paddocks where horses are kept. Rounding the corners of the field makes it less likely for a horse to injure himself when galloping about, either by coming to an abrupt halt (with the possibility of jarring the legs) or actually crashing into the boundary. Acute corners can also be traps for a timid horse who might find himself literally "cornered" by a more aggressive companion.

the horse banging into the posts when galloping about and also prevents him from pushing a rail off if he leans or rubs against it.

A tall, thick **hedge,** provided it is without poisonous trees or shrubs, can also make a good boundary. Beech and hazel are particularly suitable since horses will not eat them. Unlike a fence, a hedge provides horses with shelter in bad weather. It will, however, require regular trimming to keep it in good order – if gaps begin to appear they must be fenced off.

Probably the best boundary of all is a combination of the two: a good dense hedge with a post and rail fence running immediately in front of it.

Cheaper, less attractive but equally effective fencing can be constructed with **wire mesh**. The mesh must have small, V-shaped openings so that there is no possibility of a horse catching his foot in the holes. Mesh fencing needs to be erected professionally to prevent sagging. It is also likely to stretch when leant on.

Plain wire fencing will provide a good horseproof barrier so long as it is well constructed. It should consist of four or five strands of wire attached to stout wooden posts, with strainers at the corners to keep them taut. An alternative, and one which makes the fence more easily visible to the horse, is to use a wooden rail in place of the top strand of wire. The strands of wire should be some 12 inches (30cm) apart and the placing of the lowest strand is particularly important. It should be about 18 inches (46cm) above the ground. Any lower and the

horse may put a leg through the strands and become caught up; any higher and he may be tempted to put his head underneath. Plain wire is more suitable than barbed wire. If the latter cannot be avoided, it must be kept absolutely taut – loose barbed wire can cause dreadful injuries if any part of the horse becomes caught up in it. Horses can also cut themselves if they rub against the barbs.

Gates

Good access to fields is most important. Gateways must be wide enough to allow not only horses to pass through safely but also large machinery (such as a tractor and harrow) which will be required from time to time to keep the pasture in good condition. For safety's sake it is better for gates to be situated away from busy roads. Wooden and metal gates are both suitable for horse paddocks. All gates should have cross bars for added strength.

It is best to have a gate hung by an expert to ensure that it does not sag, drag on the ground or swing. Gates must open easily otherwise a horse could try to push his way out while you are still struggling to open it. The safest way to hang a gate is so that it opens inwards into the field. This will

SAFETY CHECKLIST

- Make regular checks of all gates.
- Replace/repair worn or damaged catches/hinges immediately.
- Keep gates securely fastened, using chains and padlocks at BOTH ends.
- Never fasten gates with bits of rope or string – horses can bite through them and they are easily removed by thieves.
- Avoid gates less than 6 feet (1.8m) wide – horses can easily bang themselves, especially their hips, as they go through.
- Avoid gates that open directly on to a main road – it is dangerous leading a horse straight out into traffic and will also make theft easier.
- Never use flimsy metal gates – they are too easily bent and broken.
- Avoid rusty metal gates – horses can easily injure themselves.
- Avoid straining gates by climbing over them.
- Avoid feeding horses close to the gateway – the ground will quickly become poached in winter.

■ BELOW
Gate posts must be strong. Gates should be securely fastened at both ends with sturdy chains and padlocks.

prevent a horse pushing it open as soon as you unfasten the catch. A wooden gate should be heavy and solidly built and, like fencing, should be treated with preservative.

■ BOTTOM
This broken gate is totally unsuitable for a paddock. Rusty metal may cause serious injuries and flimsy barriers encourage horses to escape.

Galvanized metal gates will require regular painting. Gateposts need to be very strong and should be set about 3 feet (90cm) into the ground with concrete to keep them firm. They will require strong hinges and a horse-proof catch, that is one that the horse cannot unfasten with his teeth. All catches should be easy for a person to open with one hand. There should be no protruding hooks or other fastenings on which the horse could injure himself.

Horse stealing is not uncommon and so it is vital to secure all gates. Use heavy-duty chain with a strong padlock and fit one to BOTH ends of the gate so that would-be thieves cannot simply lift the gate off its hinges. Avoid climbing over gates as it tends to weaken them. If you must, always climb over the hinge end and do it quickly.

During wet weather the ground in gateways quickly becomes poached by horses being taken in and out on a daily basis or simply pacing up and down waiting to be fed. If possible, gates should be situated on well-drained ground, and not in a muddy hollow.

Shelters

In the wild, horses make use of natural shelter such as trees, banks or rocks for protection from extremes of wind, wet or heat or to escape from flies. For horses kept in the confines of a paddock it is essential to provide an equivalent form of protection. Most domesticated horses retain their natural instinct to shelter beside a good, thick hedge or under a tree rather than going inside a confining man-made structure. But not all paddocks have hedges and trees and so a wooden shelter may be the only alternative.

Since horses are happiest when kept in company with others of their kind, a field shelter needs to be large enough to accommodate the number of horses that graze together, without risk of squabbling and overcrowding. It should be positioned on well-drained ground. If this is not possible, the floor and the area around the shelter may need a hard surface, such as concrete. The shelter should be built with its back to the prevailing wind. It must be strongly constructed and treated with preservative. The roof must be sufficiently high to give horses plenty of head room (thus

avoiding possible injury) and should slope towards the back so that rainwater runs away from the entrance. Open-fronted shelters are the safest, because it is easy for a horse to escape should he be bullied by a companion. Any fixtures and fittings, such as mangers, hay racks, etc., must be strongly made and fitted at a good height from the ground, again to prevent injury. They should be checked regularly and repaired as necessary, as should the whole shelter.

Some types of smaller field shelter are designed with a bottom door which, when closed, converts the shelter into a stable. This can be very

useful if you have no other stabling but sometimes need to keep your horse or pony inside. It can also be used as an isolation box in the event of the horse contracting a contagious illness.

A less costly type of shelter may be provided by means of a wooden screen, erected in conjunction with the fencing. Windbreak screens need to be about 6 feet 6 inches (2m) high and can either be straight or double-sided, using a corner of the field. Multi-angled screens, affording protection from different directions, can be built free-standing in the open away from the fencing.

▌ TOP
A well-designed wooden field shelter with high, sloping roof, wide front opening and strong kicking boards.

▌ LEFT
This small shelter, with its narrow opening, is suitable for a single horse. With the addition of a door it could convert into a stable for emergency use if necessary.

Poisonous Plants, Shrubs and Trees

■ BELOW LEFT
Horses appreciate the shelter afforded by
mature trees such as this oak. But acorns, if
eaten in large quantities, can be poisonous so
they should be removed.

There are a good many plants, shrubs and trees which are poisonous to horses and ponies. Some, such as the **buttercup**, which are poisonous if eaten in large quantities when fresh, are not particularly palatable. On the other hand horses will readily eat yew, all parts of which are lethal. A quantity as small as 1lb (0.5kg) can kill a horse. All paddocks should be rigorously checked for dangerous plants before horses are put out to graze and regularly checked thereafter – remember that however well you tend your own grazing it can still be contaminated by seeds blowing from neighbouring land.

One of the most dangerous plants of all is **ragwort**, which is tall and easily recognized by its bright yellow

SAFETY CHECKLIST

☛ Learn to recognize poisonous plants and trees.

☛ Before putting a horse in a new paddock, make a thorough check of grassland and hedges for signs of poisonous vegetation.

☛ Dig up and burn poisonous plants.

☛ Fence off any poisonous trees which cannot be removed – make sure they are well out of reach of horses or ponies.

☛ Make regular checks of all paddocks and hedges – remember that poisonous plants can spread from neighbouring land.

☛ Never leave poisonous plants which have been dug up lying about in the paddock – many plants, notably ragwort, are far more palatable to horses when wilted or dead.

☛ Practise good pasture management: a good, dense sward of grass helps prevent poisonous plants from seeding.

☛ If there are poisonous trees in the vicinity, keep an eye open for fallen twigs or branches – particularly during windy weather.

☛ If paddocks adjoin gardens, make regular checks for cuttings dumped over the fence by their owners – they may contain poisonous plants.

☛ After using chemical weedkillers keep horses off the grass for several weeks and at least until there has been a good downpour of rain.

flowers. Ragwort contains alkaloids which poison the liver and the effects are cumulative: small doses eaten over a long period of time are just as lethal as a large amount eaten in a short time. There is no specific treatment for ragwort poisoning and the effects are usually fatal.

Ragwort can be eliminated by spraying – the best time is between late April and late May, before the flower shoots develop and while young plants are just becoming established. Or it can be dug up, though this can be hard work. All the

■ CLOCKWISE FROM RIGHT
Ragwort, yew, laurel, rhododendron and privet: all are highly dangerous to horses. Ragwort must be eradicated from horse pasture; the trees and shrubs must either be removed or fenced off out of reach.

roots must be removed from the ground and the flower heads should be burnt. Attempting to control ragwort by cutting it when it is in flower to prevent the production of seeds is unlikely to solve the problem since the plants will often grow more vigorously the following year. If a paddock is really badly infested with the plant, the best solution is to plough the land and reseed it. The better the grassland management the less opportunity there will be for ragwort to become established. The denser the sward of grass the less likely ragwort is to seed.

Foxgloves, which like ragwort become more palatable when they are dried in hay than when fresh, are also lethal to horses. As little as ¼lb (100g) may prove fatal. Symptoms of foxglove poisoning include convulsions and difficulty in breathing. A horse will die in a matter of hours.

Hemlock has a similarly disastrous effect though it takes larger quantities (around 5–10lb or 2.5–5kg) to cause death. All members of the **nightshade** family are poisonous, as is **monkshood**. **Horsetails**, commonly found growing in boggy conditions, are dangerous if eaten in large quantities in hay. Horses do not usually eat the growing stems.

Shrubs and trees to be avoided at all cost include **rhododendron** (small quantities cause death through failure of the respiratory system), **oleander**, **laburnum** (especially the seeds), **box, privet** and **laurel**. All parts of **yew**, living or dead, are lethal in small quantities – again there is no known antidote. **Meadow saffron** contains a poison which may take time to build up in the system, by which time the horse is beyond help, and the poisons present in **bracken** also have a cumulative effect which

causes poor growth, lack of co-ordination and general loss of condition. Care should be taken if there are oak trees in or around a horse's paddock. The crop of **acorns** varies from year to year. If they are eaten in large quantities, they can be harmful. They should be raked up and removed.

Plants, shrubs and trees which are poisonous to horses include:
Bracken, buttercup, flax, foxglove, hemlock, horsetail, lupin, meadow saffron, nightshade, purple milk vetch, ragwort, St John's wort, yellow star thistle
Box, laurel, oleander, privet, rhododendron
Buckthorn, laburnum, magnolia, yew
Acorns

Water

Horses and ponies kept at grass must have constant access to a clean supply of water. A natural supply of running water, such as a stream or river, is ideal but nowadays it is all too likely that it may be polluted. If it is not, then horses and ponies may be allowed free access provided the bottom is gravel (if it is sandy the horse may ingest sand with the water).

The approach to the drinking area must be clean, fairly flat and safe. Steep banks are not suitable since the horses will slip and slide down and the bank will eventually collapse. If the stream is narrow, this could arrest the flow of water. Any fencing that crosses the stream or river must be checked regularly to ensure that horses cannot escape from their paddock by wandering off along the waterway. Streams which are not free flowing in summer are not suitable, since the water will tend to become stagnant. Horses should never be allowed access to polluted rivers, stagnant ponds or boggy areas: these should be securely fenced off.

The alternative to running water is a man-made container. A galvanized water trough, purpose-built, fed by mains water and controlled by a ballcock provides an efficient water supply, although there is always the

problem of pipes freezing in winter. The feed pipe needs to be buried to a suitable depth and the length of pipe which is above ground will need to be well lagged. It is essential that the ballcock is enclosed so that horses cannot damage it.

If mains water is not available, troughs can be filled by hosepipe or, if convenient, by bucket. Troughs such as this with static water will require baling out every week and refilling. Smaller containers, such as old stone sinks, plastic tubs and buckets can also be used but they will need more frequent filling. The advantage of small, lightweight containers is that they are easy to clean and they can be moved about to different areas of the field to prevent wear and tear on the ground. The disadvantage is that they are easily

knocked over. Standing a bucket or tub in an old car tyre is one solution to this problem.

Water troughs are best positioned parallel to a fence. Horses drink a lot so the approach to a trough will be in constant use. It should be hard – it may be necessary to lay concrete or hard core.

SAFETY CHECKLIST

- ☛ Check your horse's water supply every day.

- ☛ Bale out and clean all water containers regularly.

- ☛ During severe weather be prepared to break ice on water two or three times a day.

- ☛ Fence off all sources of stagnant water.

- ☛ Never place a water trough in the corner of a field where a horse may be trapped by one of its companions.

- ☛ Never place a water trough under deciduous trees or near a hedge where leaves, twigs and seeds can foul it.

- ☛ Avoid placing troughs in the middle of fields where they can become a source of injury.

- ☛ Recess water troughs into the line of the fence to minimize projections and the risk of injury.

- ☛ Never place a water trough slightly in front of a fence so that a horse could trap his leg between it and the fence.

- ☛ Avoid using containers such as old baths that have rough edges or dangerous projections.

Grass Management

Careful management is required if a paddock is to withstand the horse's close-biting method of grazing and the constant wear and tear inflicted by his feet. Poor quality grazing quickly becomes "horse sick" – barren areas alternate with patches of intrusive, unpalatable weeds such as nettles, docks and thistles – and without a good grass sward it will also become badly poached in wet weather. Even good quality grazing will deteriorate if it is not given the right attention.

The ideal pasture is one that has been sown with seed selected and mixed specifically with horses in mind. A good basic mixture would contain 50 per cent of perennial rye grass, 25 per cent of creeping red fescue and 25 per cent of a mixture including crested dog's tail, meadow grass and a little wild white clover. Timothy should also be included if you intend to take hay from the paddock.

Rye grass grows well in most conditions although on poor, light soils it will decline after a few years if it is not fertilized. Two different types should be included in the mix. Creeping red fescue is particularly useful in difficult conditions (it is often used on sports grounds) and again two different types should be included. Smooth-stalked meadow grass will grow in dry, sandy soils while the rough-stalked variety, which horses find very palatable, thrives in moist, rich soils. Its dense, low growth helps prevent the intrusion of weeds and poisonous plants. Clover is useful because its root nodules contain nitrogen-producing bacteria. Its inclusion in the mix will help reduce the need for fertilizing. It is important to choose wild clover rather than one of the farm varieties, which grow very aggressively and can take over an entire paddock.

Even with the right basic mixture of grasses, the amount and quality of grazing produced will vary according to a number of natural factors. These include soil type, rainfall, wind and altitude. Soil should be tested for its

suitability to sustain grass. For example, if it is acidic it will need to be treated with lime (horses must be kept off the grazing until the lime has been washed in by rain).

The best grazing is produced on well-drained land. The installation of underground drainage is expensive but it may be essential where ground is so badly drained that it is both unproductive and easily poached by a horse's feet. Where drainage exists it is important to maintain it. Check ditches regularly, and remove any blockages which prevent water from running away freely (remember that blocked ditches on neighbouring land can prevent the free run of water from your paddock). Check all pipes leading into and out of ditches and repair as necessary.

Ideally the horses' droppings should be removed frequently as this will help to control worm infestation. Where removal is not practical, for example on large acreages, the droppings should be harrowed regularly. This should be done during warm, dry weather (which will spread out the droppings and kill the larvae). Another aid to worm control is the grazing of cattle either with the horses or in rotation. The larvae will be destroyed in the cattle's digestive system. Cattle and sheep will also help keep paddocks tidy by eating the rougher herbage. Sheep do less damage to wet ground than cattle.

Harrowing in the spring helps to pull out dead growth and make room for new, and a field should always be harrowed before the application of fertilizer. Rolling will help to firm the soil and repair poached areas. Weed control is also best carried out in spring as soon as new shoots appear. Persistent weeds should be dug out and burnt before they seed.

Pasture needs to be rested periodically. If you have nowhere else to put your horse, divide off the paddock into two or more sections. Rest one portion, graze horses in another and, if possible, graze cattle or sheep in a third.

THE STABLED HORSE

Well-designed stabling is vitally important to the horse's health and safety, whether the horse lives in most of the time, whether he is kept on the combined system (that is part stabled, part out at grass) or whether he is stabled only occasionally.

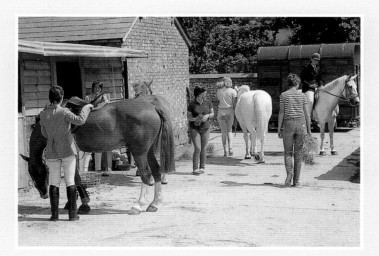

▮ O P P O S I T E All stables should have horse-proof fastenings on the outside of the doors.

▮ A B O V E Roughened concrete provides a suitable surface for a busy stableyard.

Stables

Care must be taken with the positioning and construction of stables. This applies equally to a single stable and to a large yard. Stables should be sited so that cold north and east winds cannot blow in and should be positioned on well-drained ground. When planning new stabling, various factors should be taken into consideration. These include the supply of water and electricity as well as vehicular access. It is preferable, too, to build stables near a house, in order to deter thieves.

The most popular type of stable is the loosebox, or box stall. These are usually made of wood, concrete blocks or brick and may be roofed with wood (protected by waterproof felt), tiles, slates or heavy-duty corrugated plastic. Metal should never be used for stabling because it is hot in summer and cold in winter; it is also likely to cause injuries to the horse. A loosebox must be large enough for the occupant to be able to move about, roll, lie down flat and get up again in comfort and absolute safety. A horse standing 16hh and over needs a loosebox

▮ BELOW
Good airy barn stabling provides a suitable alternative to looseboxes, especially in a hot or very cold climate. The disadvantages are the ease with which disease can spread and the fire risk.

measuring at least 12 feet x 14 feet (3.7m x 4.3m); a horse up to 16hh, 12 feet x 12 feet (3.7m x 3.7m), and a 14hh pony, 10 feet x 12 feet (3m x 3.7m). A stable of 8 feet x 8 feet (2.4m x 2.4m) is adequate for small ponies.

The roof should be sloped and fitted with effective guttering and downpipes. A high ceiling or roof is essential to prevent the horse hitting its head. If the stable has a ridge roof, the eaves should be no less than 7 feet 6 inches (2.25m) above the ground and the top of the roof should be from 12–15 feet (3.7–4.5m) high. The lowest point of a single-planed roof should be no less than 10 feet (3m) high.

Wooden kicking boards, to a height of at least 4 feet (1.2m), provide added strength and security. The stable floor should slope slightly towards the rear of the box (to aid drainage) and the surface must be hard-wearing and non-slippery. Roughened concrete is most often used. It may be covered with a special rubber material to give better purchase. Drains inside the stable are best avoided as they tend to become blocked with bedding and can also trap a horse's hoof.

For safety, the stable door must give plenty of clearance – it should be at least 4 feet (1.2m) wide and 7 feet (2.1m) high for a horse. It should be made in two halves, opening outwards, and the top half should fasten back securely for the free circulation of air and to enable the horse to see out. Only rarely is the weather so severe that it is necessary

■ OPPOSITE TOP
A well-built block of brick stables. The overhang gives extra protection to horses and humans from extremes of weather.

■ OPPOSITE MIDDLE
Note the protective strip on the top of the doors and the kick-over bolts at the bottom.

■ BELOW
The inside of a barn complex. With kit and equipment conveniently to hand, this type of stabling is popular with humans though it can be a boring environment for horses.

■ BELOW
A converted container makes a poor and potentially dangerous home for a horse. Metal is cold in winter and hot in summer and the horse could easily injure himself on the makeshift door.

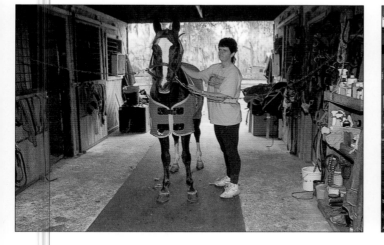

SAFETY CHECKLIST

☛ Provide adequate fire extinguishers (water and foam)/fire hose/sand buckets in the stable area – your local fire prevention officer will advise on suitable precautions. Have fire extinguishers serviced regularly.

☛ Ensure that all electrical wiring is protected with suitable conduits to prevent interference by horses and rodents.

☛ Ensure that all light fittings are out of reach of the horse.

☛ Fit waterproof switches, well out of reach of the horse.

☛ Keep stable fixtures and fittings to a minimum: two rings, one to tie up the horse, one (if required) for a haynet; water bucket or automatic waterbowl; manger.

☛ Make regular checks for protruding nails, screws, splinters etc.

☛ Make regular checks of all door bolts and hinges and keep them oiled.

☛ Fit protective grilles to all windows.

☛ Keep all drains clean.

☛ Cover open drains in the stable yard area with strong grids.

to close both halves of a stable door. The top edge of the bottom door should be securely fitted with a protective strip of metal to prevent the horse chewing the wood, and the door should have a horse-proof bolt at the top and a kick-over bolt at the bottom.

The stabled horse needs a constant supply of fresh air, so good ventilation is essential. The open top door and high roof help provide this. What the horse does not need is a draughty environment. Windows, which help ventilate and light the stable, are usually positioned on the same side of the box as the door to prevent draughts. If they are to provide maximum air and light, they should not be obscured by the top door, which tends to be the case with some stabling. Windows must be fitted with protective grilles. Additional ventilation can be provided by means of ventilation cowls in the roof, or louvre boards in the eaves. Additional light may be provided by a window in the wall opposite the door. If this is also used for ventilation, it must be above the height of the horse's head to prevent cross-draughts.

Internal stabling, where lines of looseboxes are contained within a larger building (which can be an existing barn or purpose built), is popular in some countries and is particularly useful in areas which experience extremes of heat or cold. Correctly constructed, such stabling will be warm in winter and cool in summer, but care must be taken to provide good ventilation – infectious diseases are more likely to spread in this type of stabling arrangement. Doorways and centre aisles must be wide enough to enable horses to move about without banging themselves – sliding stable doors are often the best in this situation as they do not protrude into the gangways when open. The running channels must always be kept clean.

Another way of keeping horses under cover is the yard system, where a number of horses are given the run of a large barn or a partially covered area. The yard system is labour saving, since the horses can be kept on deep litter; and horses enjoy being together with the freedom to wander about. Care must be taken, however, to choose horses who get on with each other, otherwise biting and kicking will occur.

Bedding

An ample supply of bedding encourages the horse to lie down to rest, thus taking unnecessary strain off the legs and feet; it reduces the likelihood of injuries such as capped hocks when the horse does lie down; it allows the horse to roll in comfort and protects him from injury when he does so; it reduces the jarring effect on the legs and feet that may result from standing for long periods on hard flooring; it prevents the horse from slipping up; it encourages him to stale (male horses, particularly, are usually very reluctant to stale on a bare floor); it provides warmth and insulation from draughts and it helps to keep the horse and his rugs clean.

■ **BELOW**
Wheat straw is less palatable than oat or barley straw and is therefore the most suitable for horses.

■ **BELOW LEFT**
Deep straw, well banked up the sides of the stable, provides the horse with a safe, comfortable bed.

There are a number of types of suitable bedding, all of which have pros and cons. **Straw** has traditionally been the most popular – and economical – and many people still prefer it since it makes arguably the warmest, most comfortable bed and allows free drainage. It is normally easily available though it may become scarce in wet years. Wheat straw is the best for horses, being less palatable than barley or oat straw, both of which are also likely to contain awns which can get into a horse's eyes or irritate the skin.

Straw has the advantage of being much easier to dispose of than some other forms of bedding: it can be burnt (in a safe place, well away from stabling, hay stores, etc) or contractors may collect it for use as mushroom compost. The main drawback of straw is that it may be dusty or contain fungal spores, which can cause an allergic reaction in some horses, leading to respiratory problems. This in turn can affect the horse's work performance because he will not be able to take in enough oxygen. Coughing is often the first sign of problems in this respect.

It can sometimes be difficult finding a supply of small straw bales,

❚ BELOW
Good-quality wood shavings are a useful
alternative to straw though they provide a
rather less warm bed. They are also more
difficult to dispose of.

too, particularly if you live in an area
where there are few horse owners and
therefore not much demand for the
old type of bale. Straw is best bought
in small bales because they are easier
to handle. The large ones, weighing
half a tonne or more, are difficult to
manoeuvre and often present storage
difficulties, especially for someone
keeping horses on a small scale. It will
take about four small bales to put
down a good, thick straw bed in an
average sized loosebox and upwards
of half a bale a day to maintain the
bed, the exact quantity depending
on the amount of time that the box
is occupied.

Aside from straw, **wood shavings** are
probably the most popular form of

bedding nowadays. Correctly managed,
they provide a clean, hygienic bed
which will not be eaten by the horse.
Shavings do not have spores and,
provided they are dust free (having
been passed through a dust extractor
by the suppliers), they can be a good
alternative to straw for horses with any
sort of respiratory problem.

They are packed in strong plastic
bags and it is therefore possible to
store shavings outside, provided there
has been no damage to the wrappings
in transit. Shavings do have their
share of disadvantages, however. They
are difficult to dispose of – being slow
rotting they cannot be spread on the
land – and bales are fairly heavy to
handle. Shavings are also much

heavier to handle when wet than
straw. There is also the possibility of
foreign bodies, such as sharp
fragments of wood or nails, being
present – though this should not be a
problem with good-quality shavings.
Some horses' skin may be irritated if
the shavings are from wood which has
been treated with chemicals and foot
problems sometimes occur.

Unlike straw, which traps pockets
of air, shavings pack down closely.
A bed of shavings is therefore less
warm than a straw bed and rather
less comfortable to lie on, particularly
as it is less stable than straw and
more prone to exposing bare patches
of floor. A shavings bed will use
approximately three bales per week.

Aubiose is a fairly new and entirely natural product made from the hemp plant. It is proving particularly beneficial for horses with dust allergies and has the advantage of being exceptionally absorbent: four times more absorbent than wood shavings and twelve times more than straw. The bed is more expensive than other forms of bedding to put down initially, an average stable requiring some eight bales, but thereafter it is economical to maintain as it requires only half to one bale a week. When the bed is first laid it needs dampening with a hose or watering can to help it settle and activate its sponge-like properties.

Aubiose works by soaking up liquids in a small area at the base of the bed, in much the same way as cat litter. The top layers of the bed remain dry. It is a labour-saving form of bedding since mucking out consists simply of frequent removal of droppings and a light raking over to keep it level. It is recommended that the saturated bedding should be removed every five to ten days, depending on the horse. It is also suitable for use with the deep litter system.

Another big plus for Aubiose is the fact that it rots down to a valuable compost within five to six weeks and is therefore easy to dispose of. Its only disadvantage, apart from the initial cost, is that it is very free flowing (the particles are smaller and softer than shavings) and so it is not so easy to bank up the sides of the bed.

Shredded paper provides the most dust-free bed of all and is, as a result, often used for horses with allergies to straw or respiratory problems. It is also increasingly used for high-performance horses, such as eventers or racehorses, whose lungs need to be kept as free as possible of dust. Paper is cheaper to buy than shavings but on the other hand a deeper bed is required because it becomes saturated more quickly than either shavings or straw. On the plus side, it is light and easy to handle and provides a really

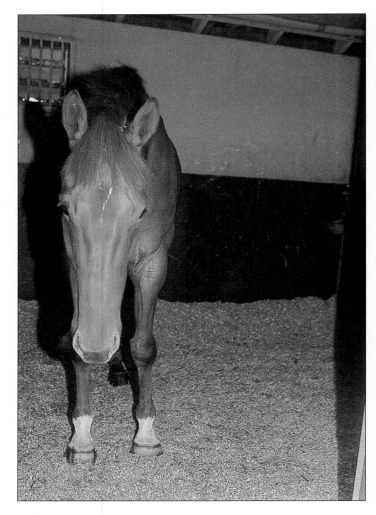

warm bed. On the minus side it is often made from printed paper and this may cause staining of the horse's coat, particularly with greys, which causes extra work for the owner or groom. It is also difficult to control a paper-bed muck heap when it is windy. Again the bed will need around three bales per week.

Peat moss may be used for bedding in areas where it is easily available . Like shavings, it is usually sold in plastic-covered bales. It, too, has its good points and its bad points. It provides a comfortable bed, is not palatable and should be reasonably

easy to dispose of. However, its main advantage over other forms of bedding is one of safety: it will not burst into flames in the event of a fire. On the other hand it is expensive, heavy to handle, needs frequent mucking out and forking over to prevent it becoming soggy and compacted and is so dark in colour that it is difficult to identify the wet areas.

Rubber matting can be used for bedding purposes but, apart from the fact that it is totally dust free when used on its own, it has more minus points than plus ones. It certainly does not look very attractive and,

■ **OPPOSITE**
Hemp is a relatively new type of bedding for
horses. It is exceptionally absorbent. Rather
expensive initially, it is economical (and easy)
to manage thereafter.

■ **BELOW**
Rubber matting is dust free, long lasting and
labour saving but affords little comfort unless
other bedding is used on top.

■ **BOTTOM**
Paper, being dust free and warm, is ideal for
bedding down horses with respiratory
problems. Printed paper can cause coat stains,
especially on grey horses.

more important, provides little
warmth or protection from draughts.
It does not absorb wet and if it is used
without a covering of other bedding
material, the droppings will be
scattered about by the horse, who will
then lie in them and, as a result, tend
always to be dirty. There is little to
prevent a horse becoming cast (the
banked-up sides of conventional beds
help in this respect). When used on
its own its chief advantage, apart
from being dust free, is its low-cost
maintenance: after the initial outlay
there is no more bedding to purchase
and the matting should last for a
number of years. Mucking out can
be done by hosepipe, and is both
quick and easy.

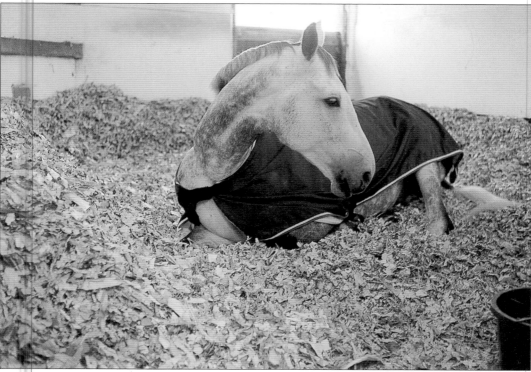

35

Management of Beds

Good management of beds is essential to keep the horse's environment healthy and to keep both the horse and his rugs as clean as possible. Stables can either be mucked out every day or you can adopt the deep litter or semi-deep litter system. The horse should be tied up during mucking out or, preferably, removed from the stable altogether. This protects him from any dust which may be disturbed while the bedding is being moved about and also makes the job easier.

Daily mucking out entails the removal of all droppings and soiled bedding. The best system is to take up the bed completely to allow the floor to dry while the horse is out. This is less of a chore with lightweight bedding materials such as straw and paper than with something heavier such as shavings.

You will need a wheelbarrow or a muck sheet, a fork and a strong yard broom with hard bristles. For mucking out a straw bed many people use a four-pronged fork for lifting droppings, but the same job can be

accomplished with a three- or even a two-pronged fork. Much depends upon the skill of the wielder – the fewer prongs, the lighter the fork, the less tiring the job and the faster you can work. For mucking out shavings you will need a shavings fork, which has more prongs set closer together. The advantage of using a muck sheet is that you do not normally need a shovel. Most of the soiled litter can be forked or swept on to it and any remnants can be hand lifted, provided you wear protective gloves. When a shovel is required, it should be large and lightweight.

The muck sheet or wheelbarrow is positioned across the doorway and visible droppings collected and placed on/in it. The bedding is cleared away from one corner of the box (usually the one on the same side as the door and furthest from where the horse is tied up, though if the box is large enough the other corners may be used in rotation to ensure that all corners of the floor are dried out regularly). The floor in that corner is then swept clean. The corner is used

to stack all the clean bedding – the squarer and neater the better since it will take up less room. All the droppings and wet straw are placed in the wheelbarrow or on the muck sheet and the entire floor is swept clean. Finally, a thin layer of the clean bedding is scattered across the box as standing litter. This will prevent the horse from slipping but will facilitate the drying of the floor. Assuming that the horse will stay tied up to be groomed and then exercised, the box can be left with the bed up for some time, which will help ensure that the floor – the sides as well as the centre – dries out before the bed is put down again.

An alternative, though not quite so satisfactory, method is to clear the bed completely from one wall of the box each day, thus ensuring that each bank of bedding is turned on a regular basis.

When putting down the bed again the existing bedding should be used to provide a good, deep covering to the entire floor area (right up to the door, to prevent draughts) and new bedding used to bank up the sides

LEFT
A selection of mucking out tools: wheelbarrow, five-tined fork, shovel, shavings scoop, broom and skip. A wheelbarrow is more cumbersome to use than a muck sheet.

ABOVE
The horse should be tied up during mucking out and setting fair. (Note that, for safety, coats should be fastened while you are working with horses.)

▮ RIGHT
A muck heap sited in a three-sided bunker is easier to manage and to keep tidy than a free-standing one.

▮ BELOW
Position the muck heap where there is good drainage and easy access – for large vehicles as well as wheelbarrows.

(with a straw bed if a horse has a tendency to eat it, new straw should be covered with a layer of the used bedding which will be less palatable). Banked sides keep out draughts, help protect the horse from injury when he is rolling or lying down and may help prevent a horse becoming cast (that is stuck with his legs in such a position that he cannot get up again).

To keep the bed as clean as possible, droppings should be picked up regularly throughout the day in a container known as a skip or skep, which may be made of metal, plastic or rubber. At evening stables the bed should be set fair, that is straightened out and put tidy for the night, care being taken to bank the sides well and ensure that the entire floor area is evenly covered.

To keep a horse on deep litter the

stable needs to be large (in a small one the bed will quickly become sodden) and well ventilated. This system saves time as it involves the daily removal of the droppings only, not the wet bedding underneath. The old bed is left undisturbed and covered with fresh bedding each day. This type of bed needs careful management and is better suited to horses who are out by day as this enables the bedding to dry out more. A deep litter bed is warm in winter and may stay down for as long as six months. However, if it begins to build up too high or to smell it must be completely removed. The box should be thoroughly dried out before a new bed is started. Woodwork will tend to deteriorate more quickly with this type of bed because of the dampness in the lower layers.

A good compromise is the semi-deep litter system, whereby the droppings and the worst of the wet bedding are removed daily and the whole box given a complete muck out once a week or once every few weeks. This works well with shavings beds. With any deep-litter system, frequent removal of droppings is essential.

Management of the muck heap is also important. For convenience it should be sited reasonably close to the stables, with a dry, level approach and easy access for large vehicles. It should be downwind of the stables. A muck heap can be free-standing or contained in a three-sided bunker – breeze blocks are particularly suitable for this purpose – which makes it easier to keep the heap tidy. Make sure that there is adequate drainage away from any paths or driveways.

During mucking out the entire stable floor should be swept clean and, if possible, allowed to dry before the bed is put down again.

The sides of the bed should be banked well up the stable walls to help keep out draughts and to prevent injury when the horse lies down.

A skip is used for the periodic removal of droppings during the day. Skips may be made of plastic, metal or rubber.

Feeds

The horse is a herbivore, that is an eater of plants and especially grass and herbs. Left to live a totally natural life, the horse will spend some twenty hours out of every twenty-four grazing, slowly moving from place to place in his search for satisfying food. Horses are what are known as trickle feeders: they have comparatively small stomachs in relation to the size of their large intestines and need to top up with food at regular intervals. In the wild they put on condition when food is plentiful and lose it when it is not. The unnatural conditions imposed upon horses by man – the lack of constant access to grass and the need to burn up energy by working – mean that they must be fed suitable alternatives to grass if they are to thrive. Feeding horses is a complex subject. Like humans, horses are individuals and vary a good deal in the type and quantity of food they need to maintain health and fitness. Basically, however, the domesticated horse's diet consists of roughage, or bulk food, and concentrates.

ROUGHAGE

The usual way to feed roughage is in the form of hay, which is simply dried grass. There are two types of hay: seed hay and meadow hay. **Seed hay** is suitable for horses in hard work, because it is usually more nutritious than meadow hay. It is taken from grasses specifically sown as an annual crop, which will include top-quality plants such as rye grass and timothy. **Meadow hay** is cut from permanent pasture and is softer to the touch and often greener in colour than seed hay. It contains a greater variety of plants than seed hay (some of which may be of inferior quality) and is usually less nutritious and therefore more suitable for animals in light work.

A newer way of feeding bulk is in the form of **haylage**, which is grass sealed in plastic bags. It comes in different nutritional levels and is particularly suitable for horses with

Seed hay (left) and meadow hay (right)

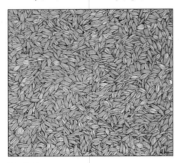

Crushed oats

Bruised barley

Flaked maize

respiratory problems. Haylage may be mixed with hay or replace it altogether as the horse's bulk feed.

Chaff or **chop** is hay, either alone or mixed with one-third proportion of oat straw, which has been chopped into small pieces by passing it through a chaff cutter. It may be added to concentrates to encourage mastication and aid digestion.

CONCENTRATES

Food such as oats and barley are known as concentrates. These are the energy-giving foods which, when fed in the correct balance with the roughage, enable the horse to perform the work required of him without losing condition.

Oats have always been considered the ideal cereal for feeding to horses. The fibrous husk covering the rich seed encourages chewing and helps prevent the horse from eating too quickly, which can seriously disrupt his digestive system. The one drawback is that oats have a low calcium-to-phosphorus ratio and the horse's diet should therefore contain a calcium supplement to balance the minerals in the roughage. Oats may not be suitable for feeding to all equine animals, however, as they can have a heating effect, making them difficult to control. Oats should be lightly rolled and used within two or three weeks thereafter, otherwise they lose nutritional value.

Barley has a higher energy value than oats but is lower in fibre. It may be fed cracked, rolled, flaked (heat treated) or micronized. It may also be fed as a mash, which is prepared by pouring boiling water over flaked barley and allowing it to cool before feeding. Whole barley should never be fed unless it has first been cooked to soften it, otherwise it is too indigestible. It should be covered with boiling water and allowed to simmer for several hours until the grain has split, swollen and become soft.

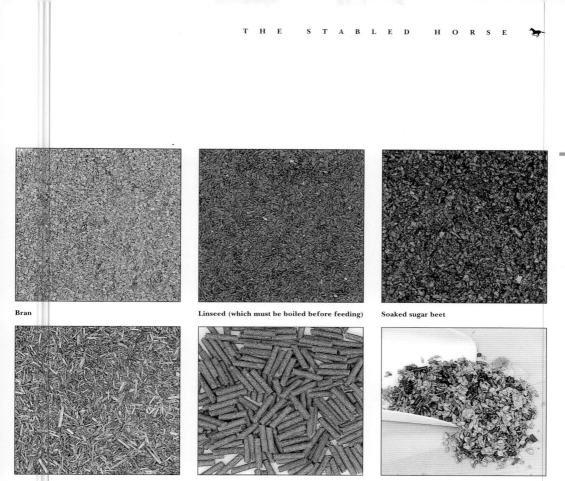

Bran

Linseed (which must be boiled before feeding)

Soaked sugar beet

Molassed chop

Horse and pony nuts

Coarse mix

Maize is high in starch but low in protein and fibre. It is usually fed flaked or micronized. It can be very heating and should be fed only in small amounts.

Bran, a by-product of wheat, is high in fibre and often fed to horses who are off work or on a low-protein diet. It may be fed dry in small quantities, mixed with the horse's other feed, or as a mash. This is made by putting the bran, together with a handful of salt, in a bucket, pouring boiling water over it (not so much that the mash is sloppy), covering and allowing it to steam and cool.

Linseed, the seed of the flax plant, is rich in oil and often fed to improve the condition of the horse's coat. It is poisonous (it contains prussic acid) if not first boiled. The linseed is covered

with cold water and soaked overnight. The following day more water is added (about 4 pints/2 litres to 2–3oz/110g of linseed) and the mixture is brought to the boil and simmered for several hours. When the resultant jelly has cooled it may be added to a bran mash or to the horse's ordinary feed.

Sugar beet is a highly digestible source of energy and fibre. It has a good calcium-to-phosphorus ratio and may be used to correct the imbalance of those elements in cereals. Sugar beet pulp (the remains of the root vegetable after the sugar has been extracted) comes in cube form or shredded. Before feeding it is essential to soak it for at least twelve hours using at least double the amount of water to pulp. Cubes may require soaking for longer in more

water. If it is not adequately soaked, it will swell up in the horse's stomach, with potentially fatal results.

Molasses is a by-product of sugar. Dark and sticky in appearance and very palatable, it may be added in small quantities to the feed to supply energy, improve the condition of the coat and to tempt fussy feeders.

Concentrates which come in cube form or as coarse mixes are known as **compound feeds**. They are made from a variety of ingredients and are scientifically prepared to provide a balanced diet. Specially formulated compound feeds are available for foals, brood mares, competition horses, and so on. They are particularly useful for the novice horseman as a good-quality compound feed takes much of the guesswork out of feeding.

Feeding

To work out a suitable feed ration for your horse you must take into consideration his size, his age, his type and the amount and nature of the work he is doing. Feeding is both a science and an art. Science tells us much about the principles of feeding and the nutritive value of the various feedstuffs but horses are all individuals and ultimately the proof of the pudding is in their appearance and performance. You can learn to judge the correct, healthy condition for a horse of a particular breed, age, size and build doing a particular job of work by studying similar animals to your own which are being used for similar purposes (perhaps at your riding school or in local competitions).

The ratio of bulk feed to concentrates will vary according to the nature and amount of work the horse is required to do. A horse in light work does not require a great deal of energy-giving feed (it will merely serve to make him a "hot" ride). On the other hand a horse such as a hunter or an eventer needs more energy-giving feed and less bulk. For a horse in light work (doing up to about six hours a week hacking and light schooling) and for most ponies the

The following is an approximate guide to total food requirements based on height (but bear in mind that it is only approximate, since horses vary a good deal in build and a finely made animal may require less food than a heavyweight doing the same amount of work):

Height	Daily feed requirement
Under 12hh	14 – 16lb (6.3 – 7.2kg)
12 – 13hh	16 – 18lb (7.2 – 8kg)
13 – 14hh	20 – 22lb (9 – 10kg)
14 – 15hh	22 – 24lb (10 – 11kg)
15 – 16hh	24 – 26lb (11 – 12kg)
over 16hh	26 – 28lb (12 – 12.5kg)

To find a more accurate yardstick it is customary to measure feed requirements against the horse's body weight (the horse requires a total daily intake of about 2–2.5 per cent of its body weight). The best way to check his weight is to use a weighbridge. Failing that you can estimate his weight by using the following formula:

$$\frac{\text{Girth}^2 \times \text{length (in inches)}}{300} = \text{weight in lbs}$$

NB Measure the girth round the largest part of the barrel at the moment when the horse has breathed out; measure the length from the point of the shoulder to the point of the buttock.

▌ **TOP LEFT**
Some barn-type stabling incorporates swinging feed bowls. They are labour saving in large yards with a lot of horses to feed.

▌ **ABOVE LEFT**
Hook-on plastic mangers are useful for feeding horses kept at grass.

▌ **LEFT**
A large corner manger is a suitable way to feed the stabled horse. Mangers must be cleaned out regularly.

GOLDEN RULES OF FEEDING

☛ Feed nature's way: little and often – the horse has a small stomach in relation to its size.

☛ Divide the concentrate ration (preferably mixed with chaff or other small roughage) into three or four feeds a day – never give more than 4lb (1.8kg) of concentrates in one feed.

☛ Feed at the same times each day.

☛ Wash mangers regularly with clean water.

☛ Never leave uneaten feed in the manger – if your horse regularly fails to eat up, either you are overfeeding or there is something wrong with him or the feed.

☛ Never feed directly before exercise – allow up to two hours for digestion.

☛ Never feed immediately after work – allow an hour for the horse to recover.

☛ Never make sudden changes to a horse's diet – introduce new feedstuffs gradually over a period of at least a week.

☛ Feed hay after concentrates and give the bulk of the hay at night.

☛ Never leave a horse for longer than eight hours without food.

☛ Always ensure that the horse has clean, fresh water available.

☛ Have the horse's teeth checked regularly – sharp edges must be rasped down to enable him to chew his food efficiently.

☛ Worm the horse regularly.

☛ Keep feed in clean, dry, rodent-proof bins, and hay in a waterproof feed shed, protected from damp ground.

☛ Add variety to the feed by giving succulents such as sliced apples and carrots (sliced lengthways to prevent choking), especially if the horse is a shy feeder.

ratio should be 30 per cent concentrates to 70 per cent bulk. For a horse in medium work (doing up to ten hours work a week, including up to two hours schooling a day, some dressage, show jumping and hacking) the ratio should be 50 per cent concentrates to 50 per cent bulk. For a horse in hard work (more than ten hours a week, or including fast work such as hunting, eventing or endurance riding) the ratio should be 70 per cent concentrates to 30 per cent bulk. These are general guidelines and all horses are different, but however hard he is working the horse should never receive less than 25 per cent bulk by weight.

Horses and ponies living out at grass during the winter require the same amount of food as stabled horses in order to maintain their health and condition during bad weather. During the spring and summer (assuming that the weather is fine) good-quality grazing should provide enough nutrition for ponies and coldblooded horses doing no more than an hour or two of light work, though it is best to check their weight regularly to make sure. During the winter, grazing will do no more than provide maintenance. In severe weather it will not even do that and the horse will lose condition if he does not receive supplementary feeding.

▮ TOP LEFT
Haynets must be tied securely and high enough to prevent the horse from catching a foot in them. Feeding hay on the ground is safer and more natural.

▮ LEFT
Horses should have access to salt, to counteract any deficiency in their diet. A salt lick is a convenient way of providing it.

▮ FAR LEFT
Soaking hay in clean water for a few hours before feeding helps prevent horses inhaling mould spores.

Water

Water makes up approximately 60 per cent of an adult horse's body weight, the exact percentage depending on his age and condition. It is present in all his body fluids and is vital for the correct functioning of the blood, the digestion and the excretion process. A horse can survive for several weeks without food but only for a few days without water.

The quantity of water required by a horse on a daily basis varies according to his diet, the prevailing weather conditions, his work load and his general health. A stabled horse may drink in the region of eight gallons (37 litres) of water a day, although the amount may be as little as five gallons (20 litres) or as much as ten (40 litres). A horse at grass may drink less than a stabled horse because of the moisture content in the grazing. A horse will drink more when the weather is hot and humid or when he sweats as a result of hard work. A sick horse may be reluctant to drink.

It is vital for the stabled horse to have access to a constant supply of fresh, clean water, the only exception being before hard, fast work. Horses are extremely fussy about the water they drink and will go thirsty rather than drink dirty or tainted water.

Water for the stabled horse may be provided either in buckets or by means of an automatic water bowl. The advantage of using buckets is that you can easily check the amount of water the horse is drinking. Water buckets should be large and strong – heavy-duty rubber is the most resilient. Plastic buckets, though convenient because they are light to carry, are not the safest as they tend to split and can cause injury. Metal buckets are stronger but they, too, might cause injury to a restless horse.

Buckets should be positioned in a corner of the stable, not right by the door but not too far from it, either, so that they are easy to reach for refilling. The handle should be positioned away from the horse. Many horses can be trusted never to knock a

bucket over, even when it is empty. Others get into the habit of playing with theirs. Some are just naturally clumsy and will knock a bucket over when moving about the box. Water buckets can be fixed to the wall with clips or, if the stable is roomy enough, stood in a rubber tyre.

During the day water buckets should be checked and refilled regularly. Water should be replaced rather than topped up to ensure a fresh supply. At night a big horse will need two buckets so that there is no possibility of his going short. Buckets should be scrubbed out regularly with clean water.

Automatic drinking bowls, connected to the water supply and controlled by a small ballcock, are popular in large yards because they are labour saving. However, they do have several disadvantages. Compared with buckets they are quite small and may not permit a horse to enjoy a deep drink. Unless they are fitted with a plug (which should be recessed into the bottom out of the way of the horse's teeth) they are difficult to clean. Also, it is not possible to judge at a glance how much a horse is drinking. Since water consumption, like food consumption, is an indication of the horse's state of health, this is not ideal. It is, however, possible to install drinkers fitted with a meter

■ BELOW
An automatic drinking bowl provides an
alternative to buckets. The bowl must be
checked frequently to ensure that the water
supply is operating correctly.

■ BELOW
The stabled horse must have constant
access to clean water. A large horse will
need two buckets.

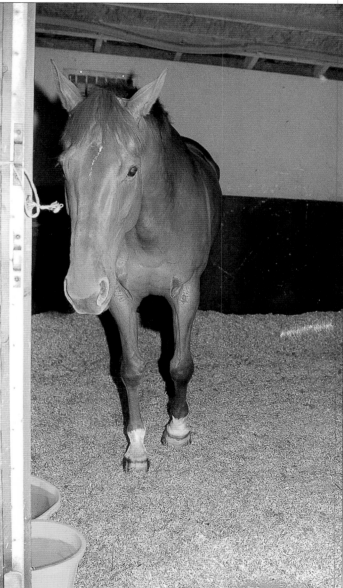

GOLDEN RULES OF WATERING

- Always provide the stabled horse with a constant supply of clean water.

- Always water before feeding.

- Never work a horse hard immediately after a long drink.

- After hard work (such as hunting or cross-country) give a horse a small quantity of water – about half a gallon (2.5 litres) every quarter of an hour until he is satisfied.

- When giving electrolytes (minerals to replace those lost during strenuous exercise) always offer plain water as well.

- Keep all water utensils clean.

- Check automatic water bowls every day.

which overcomes this problem.
All projecting fixtures in a stable
are a potential source of injury to
the horse and a water bowl is no
exception. Conversely, there is every
possibility of a bowl being damaged
by the horse. Drinking bowls must be
rigorously checked every day – a
blocked supply will cause the horse
great distress while an overflowing
bowl with swamp his bedding.
Precautions must be taken when
fitting pipes so that they cannot freeze
in winter.

Daily Care

Horses must be kept fit and healthy if they are to perform the work required of them. Keeping them that way requires daily care and attention. It is the responsibility of the owner to ensure that the horse has sufficient regular exercise of the right type and to learn how to recognize the signs of ill-health. Every horse, whether he is kept stabled or at grass, should be checked over carefully every day to ensure that he is well, sound and has no injuries or fresh lumps or bumps. Horses are creatures of habit. They thrive on a regular routine and therefore should be visited, fed, exercised and so on, at the same times each day. Some common equine ailments and minor injuries can be dealt with by the competent horseman, others will need veterinary attention. The owner must judge when to seek expert advice, bearing in mind that the sooner treatment begins, the better the chance of a cure. Regular visits from the farrier are also an essential part of horse care. There was never a truer maxim than "no foot, no horse".

Exercise

The horse needs daily exercise for the maintenance of health and, like all athletes, when he is in work he needs additional exercise to build up and maintain condition.

Where fitness of the horse is concerned exercise is always linked to feed. A horse who is kept at grass, provided the paddock is not very small, has the opportunity to take all the

■ LEFT
The stabled horse requires regular daily exercise to keep him healthy. Hacking out helps to get him fit and enables him to relax after work.

■ OPPOSITE
For racehorses, and other horses in hard work, a carefully planned exercise programme is essential.

■ PREVIOUS PAGE OPPOSITE
Most ponies, like this Haflinger, thrive when kept at grass.

■ PREVIOUS PAGE
Despite its size, the Suffolk Punch is an economical breed to keep.

■ BELOW LEFT
In their natural state, horses and ponies such as this Exmoor mare and foal have all the exercise they need.

STABLE "VICES"

Being cooped up in a stable for some twenty-two hours out of every twenty-four is unnatural and boring and may lead to a horse developing bad habits, or stable "vices". These include wood chewing, box-walking (aimless walking round and round the stable), crib-biting (in which the horse takes hold of the manger or the top of the door or some other convenient object with his teeth and swallows air) or weaving (in which he stands, usually with his head over the door, and sways from side to side). Virtually all stable vices can do harm to the horse in one way or another. All can be avoided if the horse is not allowed to become bored and frustrated.

gentle exercise he needs to stay healthy. Space and the freedom to move around at will are an intrinsic part of the horse's everyday life in the natural state so the bigger his paddock the nearer it is to his natural environment and the more contented he will be.

However, the totally grass-fed horse will not be fit to do anything other than light work in summer. By keeping the horse in a stable it is possible to monitor his food intake and gradually build up his physical fitness to enable him to carry out the work required of him. But because the stabled horse is deprived of his freedom for part, if not all, of the day a good exercise regime is essential if he is to be happy and healthy and not become unmanageable.

If possible, all stabled horses should spend part of the day turned out at grass in addition to their normal work routine. There is a danger of fit horses doing themselves harm when turned out, so it is essential to have safely fenced paddocks and to fit protective boots to guard against accidents. If for some reason it is not possible to give the stabled horse his usual exercise (for example in bad weather when it may be impossible to ride on the roads), he should be turned out for a time each day or at the very least led out and allowed to eat some grass. Another alternative to ridden exercise is to work the horse on the lunge.

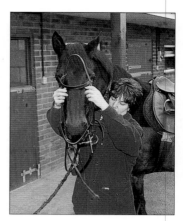

■ RIGHT
For exercise
purposes a simple
snaffle bridle and
general purpose
saddle are usually
adequate.

■ BOTTOM
Horse and rider
prepared to go. If
the horse is to be
ridden on the roads,
he should be fitted
with kneeboots.

Before being exercised or worked the horse should be given a quick grooming to make him neat and tidy. Stable stains should be sponged off and all remnants of bedding removed from his mane and tail. His feet should be picked out and his shoes checked.

An all-purpose saddle is suitable for general hacking out and roadwork. A numnah will protect the saddle from grease and dirt from the horse's coat and will also be more comfortable for his back.

Keeping a bridle for everyday use will minimize the wear and tear on the bridle you use for "best", e.g. for showing or competing. The bitting and bridling arrangement will depend on the horse. Most can be hacked out safely in a snaffle with a cavesson noseband. If you do need a little more control, you may prefer to fit a Grakle or flash noseband. Whether or not you use a martingale will again depend on the horse and how difficult or otherwise he is to control.

When exercising on the roads it is advisable to fit the horse with kneeboots – fitted correctly they will not impede his action. It is all too easy for a horse to slip up on tarmac and injure his knees, yet it is surprising how few people take this simple precaution. Brushing boots are another useful means of protecting the horse's legs.

A clipped horse in winter will need an exercise sheet to keep his loins warm. This is placed under the saddle to prevent it slipping back. It should be fitted with a fillet string, which passes under the tail to prevent it blowing up in the wind.

You can exercise two horses at the same time by riding one and leading one, in which case the led horse should wear a bridle and you should lead him either by the reins or on a leather lead rein run from one bit ring, through the other and into your hand. Never lead a horse on a lunge rein which could easily become tangled, and never wind a lead rein or reins round your hand. The ridden horse must always be between the led horse and the traffic and you should always ride on the same side of the road as the direction of the traffic.

Avoid riding and leading on roads where there is anything but light traffic and never ride and lead unless the horses are traffic-proof and well behaved. For maximum control the led horse's head should be at or just behind the ridden horse's shoulder.

For more serious work – schooling, dressage, jumping and so on – the horse should wear the saddle and bridle most suited to that activity and protective boots or bandages. For jumping, fit his shoes with appropriate studs to prevent slipping.

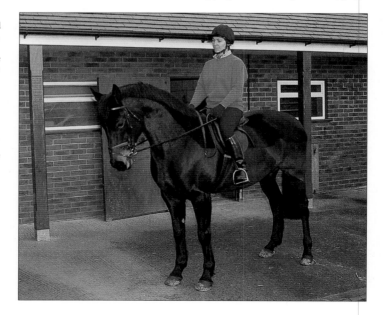

Fitness

Broadly speaking the fitness training of the horse can be divided into three distinct stages. First, there is a period of slow work designed to strengthen him up in readiness for more serious work. Second, there is the build up designed to bring him to the necessary fitness for most everyday riding activities. And third, there is the fine tuning required to bring him to a peak for physically demanding pastimes such as regular hunting, show jumping, eventing or racing.

FIRST STAGE

The period of slow work is vital and should never be rushed. The tried and tested way to make horses fit, and to prevent strains and sprains when they begin serious work, is roadwork. When the horse is first

■ LEFT
Hillwork builds up muscle, particularly in the hindquarters, and improves the horse's lung and heart capacity.

■ BOTTOM
Hacking out makes a welcome break from school work for both horse and rider.

ridden after a period of rest, he must have walking exercise only. Three-quarters of an hour a day is sufficient to begin with if the horse has been out at grass. Gradually, over a period of **two or three weeks** (preferably longer if the horse is ultimately going to be asked to do a lot of hard, fast work), this can be increased to an hour and a half to two hours a day.

Although this is slow work, the horse must not be allowed to slop along any old how. He should be kept

going forward, straight and in a good rhythm in order to start the process of building up muscles in the right places. The exercise route should be varied as much as possible to keep the horse alert and interested and he should have a day off each week to allow him to relax.

Trotting can begin during weeks **three to four**. To begin with the horse should walk for about thirty minutes before starting to trot. This will give his muscles time to warm up. His

■ **LEFT**
By week five the
horse should be fit
enough to start a
little gymnastic
jumping.

■ **BELOW LEFT**
Serious schooling
can begin when the
horse has been in
work for about
six weeks.

exercise period should also finish at walk, in order to cool him off. The trot should be controlled and rhythmic and in the early stages the periods of trot should be short and interspersed with longer periods of walk. As the days progress and the horse begins to feel fitter, the periods of trot can be made longer. The pace must always be controlled: trotting flat out on the roads (or any other hard surface) jars the horse's legs and can lead to injury. Uphill trotting is better than trotting on the flat because it reduces the strain placed on the front legs. At all times when trotting the rider should change the diagonal regularly and, when trotting uphill, keep the weight forward.

During **week four** some periods of schooling on the flat can be introduced. They should be no longer than about twenty minutes and cantering should be kept to a minimum. To encourage the horse to relax and to continue the building-up process, he should be taken for a hack afterwards.

Week five can see the introduction of a little hillwork, one of the finest ways of building up muscle. Hacking and flatwork should continue.

By **week six** he should be ready for a canter work-out, in which he should be allowed to stride on but without going into a wild gallop. As with trotting, uphill cantering is the most beneficial.

SECOND STAGE

Once the first stage in the fitness programme is completed the horse will be in a fit state to begin more serious work. Work on the flat, incorporating suppling exercises such as serpentines and circles, should be introduced. The schooling sessions should be kept short to begin with but may be gradually increased in length as the horse becomes more toned up. Gymnastic jumping exercises over grids and on circles and elements of circles will all help to improve his athleticism.

THIRD STAGE

The type of fitness required in a particular horse is always governed by the type of work required of him. For example a show jumper needs the muscular power to clear big fences but is never required to gallop flat out for a prolonged period. On the other hand the three-day eventer needs great stamina and endurance to be able to cope with the demands placed on him.

Getting the horse fit for sports which require speed and endurance involves longer periods of canter work. Canter work must be introduced gradually and should always be carried out on good ground to reduce the risk of injury. Short periods of canter are sufficient to begin with. Later, periods of long, steady cantering may be used to bring the horse to a high degree of fitness. Only rarely is the occasional really fast galloping necessary, as for instance with the fine tuning of a racehorse or three-day event horse. The main thing to remember is that the faster the pace the more chance there is of injury occurring.

Even when the horse reaches peak fitness for the activity required of him, he should be allowed regular periods of relaxation if he is not to become sour – hacks in the countryside or spells at liberty in the paddock. During a rest day after strenuous work the horse will appreciate being led out for a bite of grass.

The Healthy and the Unhealthy Horse

Recognizing signs of ill-health in the horse is all part of good horse management. The experienced horseman can tell at a glance when something is not quite right with an animal in his or her care. Learning to recognize the warning signs means an early diagnosis which, in turn, means a better chance of successful treatment.

A change in the horse's eating habits is often the first indication of something being amiss with his health: if a normally good feeder loses his appetite, be suspicious. A change in behaviour is also a reliable early-warning signal. For instance, if a normally bright, alert horse suddenly becomes listless, it may well be the first sign of a health problem. Any form of nasal discharge, coughing or a dull "staring" coat are also indications of ill-health. A change in the consistency and frequency of the horse's droppings may also mean that all is not well.

All owners should learn to check their horse's temperature, pulse rate and respiratory rate so as to know when to call for veterinary help.

The normal temperature of the healthy horse is around 101.5° Fahrenheit (38°C). You should learn to take your horse's temperature by practising while he is healthy so that you will be capable of making a fast,

The horse's pulse is to be found along the edge of the lower jaw. In the healthy horse the heart rate is about 40 per minute.

accurate reading should the need arise. The temperature is taken with a clinical thermometer which is inserted into the rectum and held there for about one minute. It is best to hold the horse's tail steady to prevent him swishing it and possibly dislodging the thermometer.

At rest the healthy horse has a heart rate of about 40 per minute. If the heart rate exceeds 60 per minute, there is definitely something wrong with the horse. To count the heart rate you need a stethoscope but failing that it is possible to count the horse's pulse rate by resting a finger over the artery situated about halfway along the bottom edge of the lower jaw. Locating the pulse will take a certain amount of practice.

In the healthy horse at rest the respiratory rate can vary from about eight to sixteen breaths a minute. To count the respiratory rate watch the horse's flanks.

Like humans, some horses have heart murmurs or faulty heart

rhythms. If a heart abnormality is only present when the horse is resting and disappears when he begins to work, there is usually no cause for alarm.

Problems with the limbs manifest themselves in various ways. Often the slightest suspicion of heat or a tiny swelling may be an indication of a serious tendon problem. Actual lameness can be detected by watching the horse as he is trotted both away from you and towards you. Watch for a sinking of the hindquarters or a nod of the head as one foot hits the ground (it will be the other limb which is causing the pain). When acquiring a new horse take note of any scars or bony enlargements so that you can distinguish new problems from old conditions or injuries.

All horses carry a worm burden which must be controlled by regular worming if it is not to cause serious damage to their health. Your veterinary surgeon will advise on a suitable worming programme.

In young horses a raised temperature and cold-like symptoms such as a nasal discharge may indicate an infestation of ascarids. These are quite large worms which can cause colic. In the adult horse the main danger comes from the large red worm, or *Strongylus vulgaris*, whose immature larvae burrow into the small arteries in the intestinal wall. The

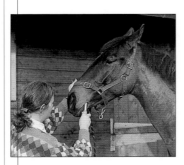

All horses carry a worm burden and require regular worming. The usual method of worming is to administer an oral paste.

The horse's temperature is taken by inserting a thermometer into the rectum. The normal temperature is about 101.5° Fahrenheit (38°C).

▌ LEFT AND BELOW
To detect lameness, watch the horse trotting
towards you and away from you. Look for a
nod of the head or sinking of the hindquarters.

damage they cause to the walls of the
blood vessels may result in a blood
clot. An infestation of *Strongylus
vulgaris* can cause colic and anaemia.
It may also disrupt the normal
movement of the bowels.

If the horse is seen rubbing his tail,
he may be suffering from pin worms,
which inhabit the rectum.

Cream-coloured eggs attached to
the horse's hair, particularly on the
legs, during summer are the eggs of
the horse bot, a fly whose larvae are
able to penetrate the skin and migrate
to the horse's stomach. If the
infestation is severe, bots can produce
ulceration of the stomach wall and
may affect digestion.

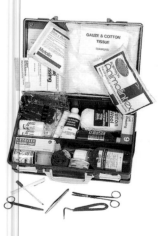

Every horse owner should have a well-stocked
equine first-aid kit readily available at all
times.

Common Ailments

Azoturia, also known as set fast or tying-up, is a stiffening up of the large muscles of the back and hindquarters. It results from the accumulation of large amounts of lactic acid. It is not always possible to determine the reason, though too much food combined with too little exercise is a common cause. The horse begins to sweat up and has difficulty in moving forwards. The muscles feel hard to the touch and the horse will clearly be in pain. Dark, red-coloured urine may be passed. The horse should be rugged up and not moved. The veterinary surgeon should be called. He or she may prescribe drugs to relieve the pain and inflammation.

In **chronic obstructive pulmonary disease** (COPD) the airways to the horse's lungs become, as the name suggests, chronically obstructed. COPD is the result of an allergic reaction to fungal spores, for instance in the horse's hay or bedding. Symptoms include a nasal discharge followed by a cough. The horse's ability to perform hard work diminishes and in time his respiratory rate at rest increases. Treatment includes rest, fresh air, antibiotics and clean stabling with dust-free bedding and spore-free feed.

Equine influenza occurs in two main strains with numerous subtypes; a serious respiratory disease, it can prove fatal. Symptoms include a horse going off his feed, a raised temperature and general cold-type symptoms. Antibiotics may help and the horse must be rested. Horses can be vaccinated, very

■ BELOW
Mud fever usually affects the lower legs. This horse also has capped hocks and windgalls (painless fluid-filled swellings just above the fetlock joints).

■ BOTTOM LEFT
The irritation caused by sweet itch often results in the horse rubbing the mane and tail hair at the affected areas.

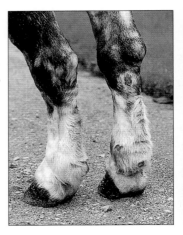

effectively, against many strains of flu – indeed vaccination is mandatory for most competition horses.

Grass sickness is a painful and fatal disease affecting the horse's nervous system. It is typified by loss of condition, muscle twitching, difficulty in swallowing and a green nasal discharge. In an acute case the horse may die in a few days. Others linger for weeks or months. Its cause is uncertain and it is more common in some regions than others.

Mud fever is a bacterial infection of the skin which affects the legs and/or lower body. It is most often seen on the lower legs. Raw areas develop which ooze serum and then form scabs. At the back of the pasterns and heels cracks often develop in the skin. The condition is most often seen in skin exposed to very muddy or very dry, dusty conditions. Skin with white hair is most susceptible. The best way of preventing mud fever and cracked heels is to protect the skin, when dry, with a barrier cream. Treatment involves clipping the hair from the affected area, regular washing (with antiseptic shampoo) and removal of scabs, careful drying and the use of antibiotic ointment.

COLIC

Colic is abdominal pain which may occur for a number of reasons, such as a sudden change in diet, migrating worm larvae, impaction of the intestines or, in rarer cases, a twisted gut. Signs of colic include the horse standing and looking round at, or trying to kick, its flank, sweating and/or repeated lying down and rolling.

The horse should be put in a stable on a deep bed to guard against injury if he wants to lie down and roll and the vet should be called. He or she may administer pain-relieving or relaxant drugs and/or a lubricant, depending on the type of colic. If a twisted gut is diagnosed, immediate surgery is essential to save the horse's life. Potentially life-threatening attacks of colic are accompanied by a high temperature (above 103° Fahrenheit/39°C) and raised pulse rate (above 60 per minute).

Rain scald is a skin infection caused by the same bacterium as mud fever. It occurs on the upper surfaces of the body. Like mud fever it is treated with antiseptic shampoos and the removal of the scabs which harbour the bacteria.

Ringworm is a fungal infection of the skin and hair. It occurs as small crusty, hairless patches and is infectious. An affected horse should, therefore, be isolated. Ringworm is treated with special antibiotic skin washes which should also be used on the horse's tack to kill off all traces of the infection. The stable should also be treated. Careful control is required as ringworm can affect humans, too.

Strangles is an infection of the lymph glands under the jaw caused by the bacterium *Streptococcus equi*. Affected horses have difficulty in swallowing and the glands under the jaw become swollen. The temperature may rise to as high as 106° Fahrenheit (41°C) and there is a nasal discharge. Infected horses must be kept warm and given soft food. Antibiotics may

help. The abscesses in the glands should be treated with hot fomentations – once they burst the horse's condition usually improves. The pus from burst abscesses is highly contagious and horses affected by the infection should be isolated. A policy of strict hygiene must be adopted to prevent the spread of the infection on clothing and equipment. Abscesses which burst internally are very serious since they can cause pneumonia.

Sweet itch is a skin irritation caused by hypersensitivity to the bites of midges and is therefore found chiefly during the spring and summer. It usually occurs along the mane and the base of the tail, which become inflamed and sore. The irritation is such that the horse will often rub out all the mane and tail hairs at the affected places, making the skin raw. A susceptible horse or pony will suffer from sweet itch annually and must be protected from midge bites by being stabled at dusk and dawn when the insects are most active. Benzyl benzoate is used to sooth the sore

areas and helps to repel the midges. Fly repellents will also help and mosquito netting should be fitted over open windows and doors while the horse is stabled. Special sheets that cover the entire neck and body give useful protection.

All horses should be vaccinated against **tetanus** and given a booster injection every other year. Tetanus is caused by a bacterium found in the soil and may enter the horse's system via a wound, especially a deep puncture wound. Typical symptoms are stiffness of the muscles, twitching, the horse standing in a stretched-out manner and, as the disease progresses, overreaction to sudden noises or movements. Eventually the horse is unable to stand and death occurs when the breathing muscles become affected. Some horses do recover from tetanus since the infection can be halted by the use of antibiotics and antitoxin. Early diagnosis is essential and the horse will need to rest in a quiet, dark stable.

Common Injuries

Back injuries, either to the bones or muscles of the back, are often the result of falls. Treatment involves rest and the use of anti-inflammatory drugs. Faradism (stimulation of the muscles by electricity), massage and laser therapy may also help.

A **capped elbow** – the term used for a bursal enlargement at the point of the elbow – is usually caused by the horse's shoe striking the elbow when he is lying down. The swelling is soft and is hot and painful when it first appears. A **capped hock** is a similar injury, caused by the horse striking his hock against something hard like the wall of his stable (perhaps through the use of too little bedding) or the partition in a horsebox (hock boots should be fitted to guard against this, particularly if the horse is a bad traveller). Unless the condition causes lameness or there is an infection, it will not require treatment. In the case of a capped elbow the horse should be fitted with a "sausage boot" (a protective ring) on the pastern. This protects the elbow while it is healing.

An **overreach** is an injury to the heel or the back of the tendon of the

front legs caused by the horse striking itself with the toe of its own hindfoot. Overreaches should be carefully cleaned. An antibiotic dressing will help guard against infection. Overreaches can be serious – there is often extensive bruising – and are often slow to heal.

Splints are bony swellings found between the splint bones and the cannon bones. Although splints are most commonly found on the inner side of the forelegs, they can occur on either side of the leg and on the hindlegs. Splints often appear when a young horse first begins work. Conformation is a contributing factor. In many cases splints are associated

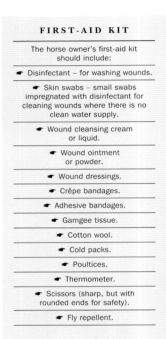

FIRST-AID KIT

The horse owner's first-aid kit should include:

- ☛ Disinfectant – for washing wounds.
- ☛ Skin swabs – small swabs impregnated with disinfectant for cleaning wounds where there is no clean water supply.
- ☛ Wound cleansing cream or liquid.
- ☛ Wound ointment or powder.
- ☛ Wound dressings.
- ☛ Crêpe bandages.
- ☛ Adhesive bandages.
- ☛ Gamgee tissue.
- ☛ Cotton wool.
- ☛ Cold packs.
- ☛ Poultices.
- ☛ Thermometer.
- ☛ Scissors (sharp, but with rounded ends for safety).
- ☛ Fly repellent.

Swollen joints can be the result of injury, infection or a dietary problem.

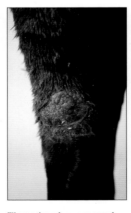

Fibrous tissue known as proud flesh may form a permanent blemish which will require surgical removal.

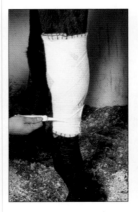

When bandaging a knee, cotton wool or Gamgee tissue should be used under the bandage.

The correct way to bandage a hock.

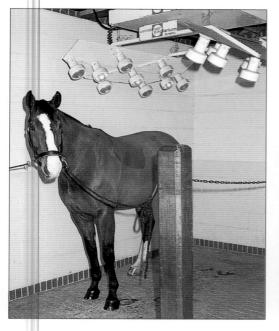

■ **LEFT**
Infra-red helps to
relax muscles and
soothe pain. This
horse is enjoying a
spell in a solarium.

■ **BELOW LEFT
AND RIGHT**
Eye injuries, such as
cuts and bruises, can
be dangerous and
require professional
attention.

■ **BOTTOM**
Stimulation of the
muscles by
electricity
(Faradism) is useful
in the treatment of
back injuries.

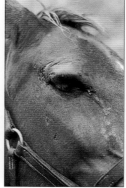

with poor foot and limb balance, in
which case corrective shoeing often
helps. Lameness may result, in varying
degrees, while the splint is forming
but often the pain associated with
splints disappears in time. In the case
of persistent lameness, the leg should
be X-rayed to eliminate any possibility
of a fracture.

Because of the strain put on the
legs when galloping and jumping,
tendon injuries are all too common
in horses, particularly in the forelegs.
The superficial and deep flexor
tendons, which run down the back of
the cannon bones, the suspensory
ligament, which is immediately
behind the lower part of the cannon
bone, and the check ligament,
situated below the knee, are all at risk.
Tendon and ligament injuries are the
result of sudden stress, which causes
the fibres to tear. The injury causes
pain, followed by heat and swelling.
Cold is the most important part of
the treatment: ice packs or, in an
emergency, a pack of frozen peas,
should be applied to the site of the
injury as quickly as possible. Ice packs
should be replaced frequently and
the limb should be bandaged firmly,
though not too tightly, for support.
Laser treatment may help to reduce
the swelling. The oldest – and best –
treatment for all strains and sprains

is rest. A leg which has suffered a
serious tendon injury is more likely
to stand up to future work if the
horse is given a period of twelve to
eighteen months off. The veterinary
surgeon can determine, by using
a scanner, when a tendon injury
has healed.

Horses suffer all types of **wounds**
as a result of falls, accidents in the
field and stable, and bites and kicks
from other horses. Some, such as
grazes, heal quickly provided they are
kept clean and dry. Others can cause
serious problems. **Puncture wounds**
are often the most dangerous since
bacteria may be carried deep into the
wound. Although it is impossible not
to notice a large, jagged laceration
accompanied by a copious flow of

blood, it is easy to overlook a deep
puncture wound simply because the
wound to the skin is small and
insignificant looking. It is important
to ensure that such wounds heal
from the inside out – poulticing
may be necessary to draw out
infection.

All wounds should be cleaned, if
possible, with cold water though it
should be remembered that
continuous washing will not stop a
wound from bleeding. The
application of a pressure pad (such as
a clean handkerchief) will help
control the flow of blood while you
are waiting for veterinary help. Large
wounds may need stitching. If there is
any doubt about the horse's
vaccination status, he must be given a
tetanus injection. If a wound needs
covering to keep it clean, medicated
gauze should be used as it will not
stick to the wound. Wounds on the
body, where the skin is loose, heal
better than leg wounds which tend to
develop proud flesh as they heal.
Proud flesh is fibrous tissue,
projecting beyond the level of the skin
surrounding the wound and often
forming a permanent blemish. The
veterinary surgeon may advise using
caustic preparations to arrest its
development or it may need to be
removed surgically.

Poulticing and Cold Treatments

The application of heat by means of a poultice helps to repair injury by stimulating the blood supply to the affected area. Heat also has a "drawing" effect, and will help to bring any pus to the surface.

Poultices may be made with kaolin, or specially impregnated padding can be bought. To make a hot kaolin poultice the tin of kaolin, with the lid loosened, is placed in a pan of boiling water for several minutes. When the kaolin is hot (no hotter than can be borne on the back of your hand) it is spread over a piece of lint, covered with gauze and applied to the injured area. To keep the heat in, polythene or aluminium foil is then wrapped over the gauze, followed by a piece of Gamgee tissue and the poultice is held in place with a bandage.

The poultice should be changed at least twice a day. All the kaolin must be removed from the wound before a new poultice is applied, otherwise the drawing effect of the new poultice will be lost. The main drawback of kaolin is that it is messy to put on and remove. This problem can be

overcome if you use ready-made poultices consisting of kaolin enclosed in a thin envelope of polythene.

Gamgee-type tissue impregnated with chemicals with drawing properties is also available. This must be activated by soaking in warm water. Like the envelope type of kaolin poultice it is easy to apply though it does leave a residue on the skin which

must be cleaned off before another poultice is applied.

Bran may be used to poultice the horse's foot in the case of problems such as a septic foot or corns. Boiling water is poured on to one or two scoops of bran to form a crumbly, not excessively wet, mixture. Test the bran for heat on the palm of the hand before applying it to the foot. The bran may be applied in a foot poultice boot, which is strapped on to the foot, or it may be placed in polythene and sacking and secured in place with a bandage. Horses sometimes try to eat bran poultices so it is advisable to add a little disinfectant to the boiling water to act as a deterrent. The poultice should be left on for twelve hours.

Tubbing is used for some foot wounds, which may require more regular applications of heat. Hand-hot water is placed in a non-metal bucket or tub and the horse's foot placed in it. Horses who are unwilling to cooperate by immersing their foot should be encouraged by having hot water gently splashed on their

▌ TOP
Three types of equine boot designed to keep dressings in place on the horse's foot. Alternatively sacking, secured by a bandage, may be used.

▌ FAR LEFT
Gamgee-type tissue, impregnated with chemicals, makes an effective poultice. It is soaked in warm water before application.

▌ LEFT
Poultices should be removed at least twice a day. Any residue must be cleaned off the horse's skin before re-poulticing.

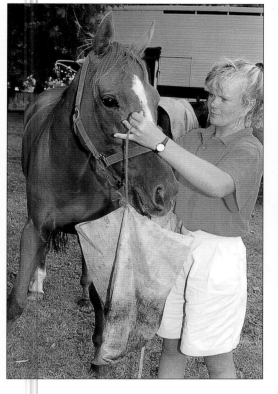

▌ LEFT
Inhalants are
sometimes used
when horses have
respiratory tract
problems. The bag
containing the
inhalant is fitted
like a nosebag.

▌ BELOW
Hosing with cold
water helps to
reduce the swelling
and heat which
accompany most
leg injuries.

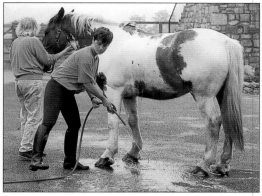

▌ BELOW LEFT
Another effective
method of applying
cold treatment: a
hosepipe attached to
a "hose boot".

▌ BELOW RIGHT
Hot or cold tubbing
can be carried out by
standing the horse's
foot in a bucket –
always providing he
cooperates!

leg. Epsom salts and antiseptic may
be added to the water. Tubbing
lasts for about twenty minutes and
should be carried out at least twice
a day.

Where cold treatment is required
as opposed to heat, there are various
methods. Cold water may be applied
with a hose for regular periods of
about ten minutes. The horse should
be accustomed to the feel of the water
by starting at ground level and then
gradually working it up the foot and
leg. The legs should be bandaged
between hosing sessions. Where
suitable facilities are available the
hose can be bandaged to the horse's
leg. He should be given a haynet to
keep him occupied. Walking or
standing a horse in a river or in the
sea is equally beneficial.

Specially designed flexible packs,
which retain their cool temperature
for quite a long time, can be obtained.
They are cooled in a freezer and
bandaged into place. Special
bandages are available, too. These are

designed to absorb water and are
flexible enough to be applied even
when the water is frozen. Another way
to apply cold to a leg is to soak
bandages in cold water (care must be
taken to remove them before they

start to dry out as they might shrink).
Crushed ice in a polythene bag or,
in an emergency, a packet of frozen
peas may be bandaged round a leg.
A thin layer of Gamgee should be
placed over the leg first.

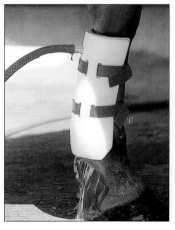

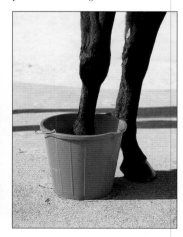

Anatomy of the Foot

Lameness in horses occurs far more often in the foot than in any other part of the limbs. This is not surprising considering the amount of strain put upon the feet of domesticated horses required to pull heavy loads or carry a rider, particularly at fast speeds or over jumps.

The term foot is used to describe the hoof – the dense horny covering – and all the structures contained inside it. The external, insensitive part of the hoof comprises the wall (the outer, protective layer of the foot); the sole (a plate of hard horn just under an inch (2cm) thick; the frog (a wedge-shaped mass of soft elastic horn), and the periople (a thin layer of epidermis between the hoof wall and the skin).

The function of the sole is to give protection to the sensitive inner structures and to help support weight. The frog performs the same functions as the sole as well as providing grip and acting as a shock absorber. The periople controls evaporation from the underlying horn.

The internal part of the hoof comprises the sensitive laminae, the sensitive sole, the sensitive frog, the periopic corium and the coronary corium.

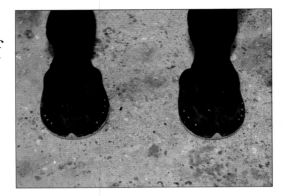

LEFT
A well-matched pair of forefeet. The toe clips steady the shoes while the nails are driven in and help to ensure an accurate fit.

Laminae are interlocking leaf-like structures which attach the hoof to the pedal bone. Hundreds of sensitive (or primary) laminae dovetail with thousands of horny (secondary) laminae which grow outwards from the interior of the wall of the hoof.

The sensitive sole, which is attached securely to the lower surface of the pedal bone, is a thin layer of tissue which corresponds to the horny sole and supplies it with nutrition.

The sensitive frog supplies nutrition to the digital cushion on which it is moulded. This cushion is a wedge-shaped fibro-elastic pad situated in the hollow behind the heels. It has an important part to play in reducing concussion by expanding when the foot takes weight.

The periopic corium or ring situated just above the coronary corium (coronary body) supplies nutrition to the periople. The coronary corium, a thick structure situated above the sensitive laminae, lies in the coronary groove and supplies nutrition to the wall of the hoof.

On the ground surface of the sole, where the sole meets the wall, is a narrow band of soft plastic horn known as the white line. This white line is of great importance to the farrier because it indicates the position of the sensitive structures of the foot and the thickness of the wall, thus helping determine where nails can be driven into the wall to hold shoes in place without encroaching on the sensitive areas.

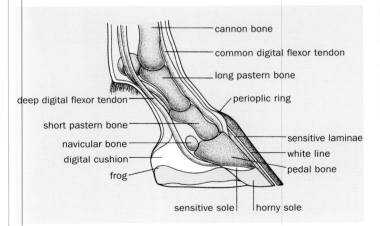

The Role of the Farrier

Horses have been shod with metal shoes for over two thousand years and although it is impossible to say for certain who first had the temerity to try nailing a shoe to the horse's hoof, it is widely assumed to have been the Celts and the Gauls.

The need to protect the feet arose when man began to use the horse as a beast of burden and for riding. The unnatural wear and tear inflicted upon the feet of the domesticated horse results in the hooves being worn down more quickly than they are renewed – this would not occur in the horse's natural state. The damage caused to the hoof is worse when travelling over hard, rough ground or in a wet environment. The latter leads to the growth of softer horn, which wears away more quickly. This explains why horses in dry, hot climates, which promote the growth of hard horn, can often do a considerable amount of work unshod without any ill effects.

The role of the farrier is of vital importance, since the horse cannot work adequately if his feet are painful. It is the farrier's job to ensure that the horse's feet are not only well and securely shod but are also correctly trimmed. The horn of the hoof is constantly growing and fitting a metal shoe to the hoof prevents excess growth being worn down naturally, as is the case with the unshod horse. The average monthly growth of horn is around ¼–⅜ inch (5–9mm) and the horse needs to have his feet trimmed about every four or five weeks, depending on the rate of growth. If his old shoes are not worn, they may be refitted – these are known as "removes".

Shoes may be fitted either hot or cold. The advantage of hot shoeing is that it ensures a better fit because the shoe can be finely adjusted to fit the foot (the shoe must always be altered to fit the foot, not vice versa). The shoe is heated in the furnace and held against the prepared hoof (which is insensitive) for a short time. The imprint it leaves indicates to the farrier any necessary adjustments required. Once these have been made the shoe is plunged in cold water before being nailed on to the foot.

It is important to remember that horses who are unshod, perhaps because they are resting, still need regular attention from the farrier. Being confined in a paddock is not the same as being free to roam in search of food, and the horse's hooves will not wear down as they would in the wild.

The farrier's work is very skilful. He must be able to trim the hoof, and drive nails into the insensitive part of the hoof wall, with great precision. One slip, and the result will be a lame horse. Nor is farriery simply about the routine trimming and re-shoeing of horses. It also involves skilled remedial shoeing, which calls for a detailed knowledge of the anatomy of the horse's limbs, including the bones, the joints, the muscles, the vascular system and the nervous system. Defective action, caused by less than perfect conformation or injury, can be greatly improved by expert trimming of the foot and the fitting of specially designed shoes. In these cases, the farrier will work in conjunction with the veterinary surgeon.

At one time it was the practice for the horse to be taken to the farrier for shoeing, which meant that the farrier had all the facilities of a permanent forge on hand. Nowadays it is usually the farrier who has to travel to the horse with a mobile forge, so the onus is on the horse owner to provide him with a suitable working area.

A dry, level surface for the horse to stand on is essential, as is good lighting. In summer, when flies are a nuisance, the horse should be in a shady area, either in a building or under a tree, and it is advisable to have some fly repellent handy.

The horse's feet should be cleaned and dried beforehand and it is the owner's responsibility to ensure that the horse is as well behaved as possible. Most horses will stand quietly. But remember that feeding or moving other horses about while a horse is being shod can make him extremely restive – and the farrier's job that much more difficult.

■ LEFT
In order to make horseshoes, the farrier must be skilled in bending, turning and shaping metal. He uses an anvil specially designed for the purpose.

The Farrier's Tools

The farrier's tools are divided into two categories: forge tools, that is those used while making shoes, and shoeing tools, that is those used while preparing the foot and nailing on the shoe.

Forge tools include the anvil, on which the metal is shaped; various hammers and tongs; the stamp, used for making nail holes in the shoes; the fullering iron, used to make a groove round the edge of the ground surface of the shoe and the pritchel, a steel punch used to finish off the nail holes and also for carrying hot shoes to the horse's foot for fitting.

Shoeing tools include hammer, pincers, trimmer and rasp. The farrier's shoeing hammer, which has a short, curved claw, is used to drive in the nails, to twist off the points of the nails and form the clenches, and to pull out nails.

When removing shoes the farrier uses a buffer (or clench cutter) to cut off the clenches or knock them up before withdrawing the nails.

Pincers are used for raising and levering off shoes and for withdrawing nails. They are also used to turn the clenches. For trimming, a hoof trimmer, cutter or parer is used. This is a tool with a pincer-like head, one side being sharp and the other flat. To remove the overgrown wall of the hoof the flat side is placed on the outside of the wall and the sharp cutting side on the inside.

When removing ragged pieces of frog or loose flakes of sole a drawing knife is used. The searcher, a similar tool but with a thinner blade, is designed for use when cutting out corns or paring away the horn round puncture wounds.

The farrier's rasp is partly coarse, partly smooth (file cut) and has serrated edges. The farrier uses the coarse side to remove excess hoof wall and for the final levelling of the bearing surface of the foot. The coarse side is also used to finish off the clenches. The file cut surface is used to finish off the shoe and to shape the clenches. Using the serrated edges the farrier removes the sharp edge of the wall (to prevent it splitting) after the shoe has been nailed on.

STUDS

Although shoes help to give the horse added grip on grass it is often essential to fit studs in the shoes as well. Studs may be permanent or of the screw-in type (in which case the shoes are provided with screw holes by the farrier). Screw-in studs are best

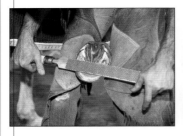

1 Having cut off or knocked up the clenches (the turned-over points of the nails), the farrier uses pincers to lever off the old shoe.

2 Excess growth of hoof is removed with a trimmer, which has one flat and one sharp side.

3 A drawing knife is used to lower the hoof wall and remove loose flakes of sole.

4 The bearing surface of the foot is levelled with a rasp before the shoe is fitted.

5 Hot shoeing ensures a better fit than cold shoeing and causes the horse no pain.

6 Nails are driven into the insensitive wall of the foot to hold the shoes in place.

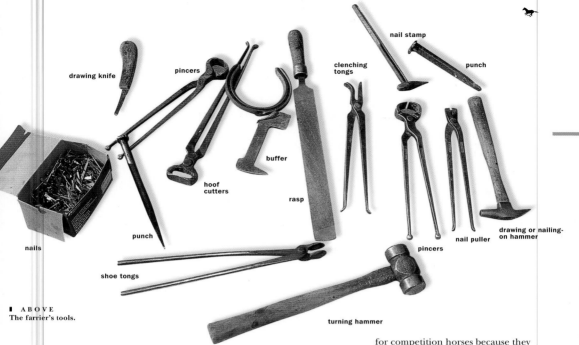

nail stamp

drawing knife

pincers

clenching tongs

punch

buffer

hoof cutters

rasp

nails

punch

shoe tongs

nail puller

pincers

drawing or nailing-on hammer

turning hammer

▌ ABOVE
The farrier's tools.

▌ RIGHT
Screw-in studs are essential for the competition horse. After use they are removed and the holes plugged to protect the threads. A T-tap (centre) is used to clean out the screw holes before inserting the studs.

for competition horses because they require different types of studs according to the work they are doing and the state of the ground.

There is a wide range of studs available, varying from small ones for everyday hacking and road work (these are usually made with a tungsten core and are very hard wearing) to large round or square ones suitable for use in soft going and pointed ones which enhance the grip on very firm ground. There are two schools of thought about the fitting of studs: some people fit only one stud on the outside of each shoe. Others believe that this may throw the foot out of balance and so fit one on either side of the shoe.

The farrier uses the rasp to smooth the horn and shape the clenches.

Lightweight plastic shoes are a modern alternative to metal ones. They are attached to the hoof with glue.

Studs are screwed into place shortly before the horse competes. The size and shape depends on the ground conditions.

Common Foot Problems

Corns occur most often in the front feet. A corn is a bruise of the sole in the angle between the wall of the foot and the bar (known as the "seat of corn"). Corns are caused by pressure and can be the result of a stone becoming wedged, faulty shoeing or shoes having been left on too long. The shoe should be removed and the discoloured horn pared away. The condition can be complicated by the presence of infection, in which case poulticing will be necessary. Pressure can be relieved from the area by fitting a shoe on which the ground surface of the heel is lowered so that it does not make contact with the ground.

Laminitis (also known as "founder") is a painful condition resulting from inflammation of the laminae. The feet become hot and the horse adopts a typical leaning back stance in order to take the weight off the front of the forefeet. Although the pathological cause is not yet completely understood, laminitis is associated with excessive concussion and the presence of inflammatory toxins which damage the blood vessels, particularly those in the feet. It is often the result of faulty diet (over-fat ponies, with overlong feet, kept on too rich pasture are the classic example) although it can also be caused by retention of the afterbirth in the broodmare.

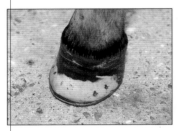

An example of the farrier's skill: this defective hoof has been artificially lengthened.

Pigeon toes (those which turn inwards) cause uneven wear on the shoes.

A sandcrack may produce lameness if the sensitive part of the foot is affected.

Veterinary treatment is essential. If diet is the cause, the vet may advise a purgative. The horse should be stabled (standing the horse on sand is said to reduce the pain because it provides support to the feet). The vet may prescribe drugs (including pain killers) and if the horse or pony is overweight, he will advise on a suitable diet.

One of the dangers of laminitis is the possibility of pedal bone rotation. Except in the mildest cases, therefore, when the horse may be gently led out in hand, the horse must be given box rest.

Good foot care is vital. Corrective trimming will help restore the structures of the foot to their normal alignment and will limit the rotation of the pedal bone. Special shoes can also be fitted.

Navicular disease is believed to be the result of poor foot conformation and/or concussion, caused by hard work. Bony changes occur in the navicular bone, a small, shuttle-shaped bone which acts as a fulcrum

This leaning back stance is typical of a horse suffering from painful laminitis. He takes the weight on his heels to relieve the pain.

Laminitis is one of the major causes of equine lameness, particularly in overweight horses and ponies.

for the deep flexor tendon before the tendon attaches to the under side of the pedal bone. In most cases both forefeet are affected.

A horse with navicular disease will put his foot on the ground toe-first as he attempts to avoid pressure on the affected area. In the early stages, lameness wears off during exercise but as the condition progresses the periods of lameness both increase and become more prolonged. As time

centre of the pastern (high ringbone) or around the coronet (low ringbone). It is usually caused by injury. There is heat and swelling and the horse may have a shortened stride and tend to be more lame when turned sharply. Rest may help give relief in less serious cases. Where more serious injury is involved the horse may not become fully sound again, although some horses continue to work if given anti-inflammatory drugs.

be the result of bruising of the toe area or pressure from the toe clip of a shoe. Sometimes it follows laminitis. Treatment involves cleaning out the cavity and filling it with tow. The farrier will be able to trim the foot and shoe it in such a way that further damage is avoided during movement.

A **sidebone** results when the lateral cartilages of the foot become ossified or converted into bone. The ossified

"Boxy" feet have an angle of more than 55° and are associated with upright pasterns.

Shoes with rolled toes reduce strain on the tendons and the navicular bone.

A plastic wedge raises the heel of a hoof which slopes too much.

goes on, the horse may become prone to stumbling.

Although the condition is incurable, various treatments are employed to help relieve the pain. Corrective shoeing is used to raise the heels and reduce concussion to the navicular area. The horse may be given anticoagulants or anti-inflammatory drugs. Laser and ultrasound treatment may also be beneficial.

Pedal osteitis is inflammation of the pedal bone. It is often the result of jarring but can also develop after an attack of laminitis or following puncture injuries to the sole of the foot. It usually affects both forefeet and the horse will tend to shuffle when he moves. The demineralization of the bone is visible on X-ray. Careful shoeing can bring relief to what is usually an irreversible condition. Laser and ultrasound therapy may be beneficial.

Ringbone is an abnormal bony growth which occurs either at the

A **sandcrack** is a break in the wall of the hoof and may occur anywhere between the coronet and the ground surface of the foot. Sandcracks may be the result of injury, poor nutrition, an overdrying of the hoof (for instance in very dry weather), too much rasping during the shoeing process or neglect, for example lack of regular trimming by the farrier. Lameness may result if the crack is serious.

The farrier may be able to arrest the progress of a sandcrack by making grooves in the hoof wall to isolate the crack. Metal clips may also be used or, in the case of a deep crack, it may be necessary to fill it with a special bonding substance. Because the crack opens when weight is put on the foot as it is placed on the ground, a shoe with clips may be fitted.

Seedy toe is a condition in which the wall of the foot parts company with the sole at the white line. It may

cartilages can be felt at the junction of the hair and the hoof in the area of the quarter of the foot. Sidebones are usually caused by concussion. Heavy or common-bred horses are the most susceptible. The horse may be lame while the cartilage is ossifying and sometimes lameness persists once the sidebones have developed because of pressure on the wall of the foot. The condition does not normally require treatment other than short-term rest but if lameness persists the farrier may be able to relieve the pressure with corrective shoeing and grooving of the hoof to allow expansion.

Thrush is caused by bad stable management (dirty bedding and failure to pick out the feet regularly). It is easily detected by the evil smell coming from the frog, which is moist and may have a black discharge. The affected area of the frog must be opened out to expose it to the air and treated with antiseptics.

Equipment

When man first began to ride horses, his only piece of equipment was a rudimentary bridle. It was a very long time before the invention of the saddle and longer still to the arrival of the stirrup. By contrast, the array of equipment available to the modern horse owner is quite staggering: such a diverse range of bits that whole books have been devoted to their usage; saddles of every conceivable shape and size; boots and bandages to protect most parts of the horse's anatomy; rugs to keep him warm and dry, and a plethora of "gadgets" designed to control him – the majority of which would not be necessary if man made a better job of schooling the horse in the first place! For everyday riding purposes, certain items of basic equipment will suffice: a bridle, saddle, a few essential items of horse clothing. The important thing is that they should fit correctly and be well cared for, in which case they will last for many years. For the rider, the popularity of horse sports has led to the development of special clothes for each and every occasion. Everyday riding clothes should be neat, comfortable and, above all, safe. Riding is a risk sport and no short cuts should be taken in this respect.

Bridles and Saddles

The minimum basic equipment, or tack, required for the ridden horse is a saddle and bridle. He will also need a headcollar or halter and lead rope.

The simplest means of controlling a horse is by means of a snaffle bridle. There are many varieties of **snaffle bit**. The mildest is the unjointed type which acts principally on the bars of the mouth, that is the portion of the lower gums where there are no teeth. A jointed snaffle is more severe because it exerts pressure on the

■ LEFT
The double bridle employs two bits, a curb and a bridoon (snaffle). It should only be used by the experienced horseman.

■ PREVIOUS PAGE OPPOSITE
The hackamore or bitless bridle works by leverage. It, too, should only be used by the experienced rider.

■ PREVIOUS PAGE
A horse wearing a driving bridle. The blinkers prevent the horse being distracted by things alongside or behind him.

■ BELOW, LEFT TO RIGHT
A bitless bridle or hackamore; a leather headcollar; a snaffle bridle with flash noseband; a snaffle bridle with cavesson noseband and running martingale.

■ BOTTOM LEFT
Numnahs are comfortable for the horse's back. They must be kept clean – the washable type are best.

corners of the mouth as well. A snaffle may be loose-ring or eggbutt (the latter prevents the lips being pinched). The choice, as with all bits, depends very much on the horse and it may be necessary to try a number of different bits until you find the one which suits the horse best. Snaffles may be made of stainless steel, which is easy to clean and very hard-wearing, rubber, plastic or nylon. A horse with a very sensitive mouth will often go better in a non-metal bit.

The **bridle** consists of a headpiece and adjustable cheekpieces, to which the bit is attached, a throatlatch to prevent the headpiece slipping forward over the ears and a browband to prevent it slipping down the neck. There may also be a noseband. Most bridles are made of leather. Narrow leather looks best on a quality horse such as a Thoroughbred, wide leather

INTERESTING FACTS

In the United States any type of riding other than Western is known as "English". In Western riding a saddle with a high pommel and cantle is used (the design traces back to that used by the Spanish Conquistadores). The saddle is designed to give maximum comfort to the rider spending long hours on a horse.

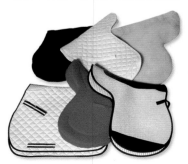

suits a heavyweight horse.

Various designs of **noseband** may be used. The widely used cavesson is fitted largely for appearance's sake – many people feel that a horse looks "undressed" without one. Other nosebands are designed to give added control over the horse, mainly by preventing him from evading the action of the bit by opening his mouth and crossing his jaws.

A **martingale** (a strap passing from the girth, between the horse's front legs, and attached to some part of the bridle) is used primarily to prevent a horse from raising his head above a certain level. A **bitless bridle** or **hackamore** may be used on a horse which is difficult to bit adequately, or one who has some problem with his mouth or teeth. The bridle works by pressure and leverage on the horse's nose and chin groove. The longer the

■ RIGHT, FROM THE TOP
A general purpose saddle; a dressage saddle; a jumping saddle; various types of girth.

■ BELOW
A selection of snaffle bits.

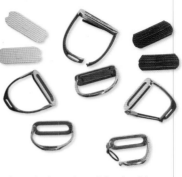

■ BELOW
Stirrup irons are made of stainless steel for strength. Treads help to prevent the foot from slipping. Safety stirrups (with one side closed by a rubber ring) prevent the foot from becoming trapped.

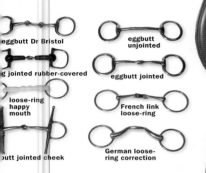

eggbutt Dr Bristol

eggbutt unjointed

jointed rubber-covered

eggbutt jointed

loose-ring happy mouth

French link loose-ring

butt jointed cheek

German loose-ring correction

cheeks of the bridle the more severe its action. A bitless bridle should only be used by an experienced rider – the braking power provided can be tremendous, but it is much less easy to make turns than with a conventional bridle.

Saddles, like bridles, have traditionally been made of leather, though nowadays cheaper, synthetic ones are also available. All saddles are built on a tree, or frame, made of laminated wood, with inset springs for added resilience, or of plastic.

For everyday use an all-purpose saddle is suitable, being designed as its name suggests for general riding. For riders specializing in dressage or show jumping there are saddles designed for the job. The dressage saddle has a deeper seat and straighter flaps than the all-purpose saddle, allowing the rider to use a longer length of stirrup and to have more of the leg in contact with the horse's side. The jumping saddle is made on a longer tree and has forward-cut flaps to enable the rider to ride with short stirrups and to adopt the necessary forward position.

Stirrup irons should be made of stainless steel for strength and must be large enough to allow a gap of about ½ inch (1.5cm) on each side of the rider's boot. Good quality **stirrup leathers** are essential for safety.

It is vital that the saddle fits both the horse and the rider. It must not

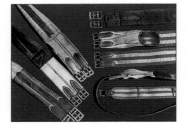

impede the action of the shoulders and there must be no pinching of the withers or pressure on the spine. The rider's weight should be evenly distributed on the large muscles on either side of the spine. An incorrectly fitted saddle will result in a sore back. The rider's shape and length of leg must also be taken into consideration as it is impossible to ride well on an uncomfortable saddle.

The saddle is held in place by a **girth** or girths, the design of which will depend on the horse's conformation, the type of saddle and the type of work being done. Girths were traditionally made of leather, but today they are also available in synthetic materials.

A **numnah**, or saddle pad, fitted under the saddle, affords greater comfort to the horse than the leather lining of the saddle. The numnah should be made of natural fibre which will absorb sweat. The centre must be tucked up well into the channel of the saddle to prevent pressure on the spine. Numnahs must be washed regularly – dirt can cause a sore back.

To guard against the saddle slipping back the horse may be fitted with a **breastplate.** The leather hunting breastplate has straps which are attached to the D rings of the saddle. The racing breastplate, also known as the Aintree type, is a broad band of web or elastic which passes round the horse's breast and fastens to the girth straps.

Rugs

Regular grooming deprives the stabled horse of the natural protection of grease and dirt which, in the wild, accumulate in his coat and help to keep him warm. In winter clipping removes even the natural protection of a woolly coat. It is most important, therefore, that the stabled horse is provided with rugs and blankets, the amount depending on the individual horse and the prevailing weather conditions.

The traditional type of stable rug or night rug is made of hard-wearing jute, lined with wool. It fastens round the horse's chest and should be kept in place with a roller rather than a surcingle, which can cause pressure on the spine. A roller is a broad strap, padded where it lies on the horse's back (with a clear channel for the spine) and fastened with two strong buckles. Leather rollers are very hard wearing though they are heavier than the webbing variety. If necessary a breast strap can be fitted to prevent the roller sliding back. Wither pads fit under rollers and are designed to give added protection from pressure. All rollers should be regularly checked,

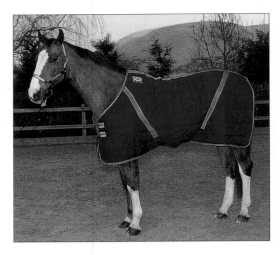

■ LEFT
A lightweight stable rug with fitted surcingles which eliminate the need for a roller.

particularly the stitching, as they take a great deal of strain when the horse gets up or down and when he rolls.

Stable rugs also come in a range of modern materials, which are lighter to handle than jute and may be fitted with self-righting straps (that is they will return to the correct position on the horse even if he rolls), which eliminate the need for a roller.

For added warmth a blanket or blankets may be fitted under the stable rug. The traditional type is the Witney blanket, made of wool and coloured gold with red and black stripes. To prevent the blanket

slipping back it is positioned high up the horse's neck. The corners are then turned up to the withers. The rug is placed on top, the front of the rug fastened and then the folded part of the blanket is turned back over the top of the rug and the roller fitted on top of both the blanket and the rug. A cotton sheet may be placed under the blanket to keep it clean (blankets do not usually wash well). Where no roller is used it is difficult to keep a blanket in place and better to use a specially designed quilted liner under the rug for extra warmth.

Day rugs are usually made of wool

■ RIGHT
New Zealand rugs are ideal for horses when turned out in cold or wet weather. A carefully designed system of leg straps ensures that the rugs stay in place even if the horse rolls.

RUG CARE

- ☛ Check all fastenings regularly and have worn stitching repaired – leather straps with buckles are the strongest type of fastening and the easiest to use.

- ☛ Keep all leather fastenings soft and pliable and all buckles and clips oiled.

- ☛ Give all rugs, blankets and sheets a daily shake and, if possible, an airing.

- ☛ Give all washable rugs and sheets a regular wash in a safe washing powder (some horses are sensitive to biological powders) and dry well before re-using or placing in storage.

- ☛ Give jute rugs a regular brushing – scrub thoroughly as necessary.

- ☛ Give woollen rugs and blankets a thorough, regular brushing – have them dry cleaned as necessary.

- ☛ Check the stitching and buckles on rollers regularly.

- ☛ Clean the outside of New Zealand rugs with a hose and brush – detergents may damage the waterproofing – and scrub the linings.

- ☛ Have New Zealand rugs reproofed as necessary.

- ☛ Protect stored rugs from moths.

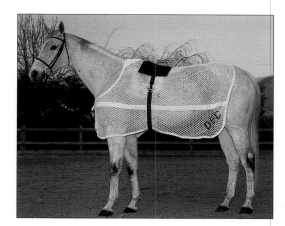

▌ RIGHT
A string rug is useful to help dry off a wet horse. Note the surcingle fitted over a back pad to prevent pressure on the spine.

(different weights are available for use in winter and summer) and are most often kept for use on special occasions such as at shows and other public appearances.

Cotton sheets are suitable for use in summer when they will give protection from flies and also help to keep the horse clean. Cotton mesh or string rugs are used to help dry off a sweaty or wet horse. In cold weather a sheet may be placed over the top to prevent chilling. All sheets should be kept in place with a surcingle, preferably fitted over a back pad. Light cotton coolers, which cover the horse from just behind the ears to the top of the tail, are useful in hot climates to protect the horse from both sun and flies.

When travelling, the horse should always wear rugs made of a breathable material to ensure that moisture can escape should he become sweaty.

Horses who are turned out for part of the day and some who live out permanently will need a New Zealand rug. New Zealand rugs are warm, waterproof and windproof. They may be made of heavy canvas (which can cause pressure sores) or lighter weight modern weatherproof materials. To give adequate protection the rug must be well shaped and come well down the legs and over the quarters. Some rugs have tail flaps and neck covers for added protection in really bad weather. Correct fit is essential to enable the horse to move about freely. New Zealand rugs are fitted with a system of leg straps and many are self-righting. All straps must be kept clean, soft and supple to prevent chafing of sensitive areas such as the insides of the legs.

For exercise purposes the horse may need a paddock sheet to keep his loins warm. A paddock sheet (so named because they are traditionally used on racehorses) does not have a front fastening but is fitted under the saddle, usually with the corners turned back. A fillet string passing under the tail helps prevent the rug blowing about on a windy day. Paddock sheets are usually made of wool or cotton but they are also available in waterproof materials. A fluorescent sheet is an excellent safety device for use when riding on the roads.

Waterproof rugs and sheets are particularly useful at shows and competitions for keeping tack and other rugs dry. Since most waterproof materials do not "breath" care must be taken that the horse does not sweat up when wearing this type of rug. Remember, too, that noisy materials can startle horses.

▌ RIGHT
The leather covered metal hoop on this anti-cast roller helps to prevent the horse from rolling over in his box and becoming cast (stuck). The roller should be fitted over a back pad.

Bandages

Leg bandages may be used to give protection, support or warmth, as required. Exercise bandages are made of crepe or stockinette and may be used instead of boots to give protection and support to the tendons. They are about 3–4 inches (8–10cm) wide and should be put on over a layer of Gamgee or other suitable padding.

Bandaging the legs is a skilled task and should not be attempted by the novice horse owner except under expert guidance. Exercise bandages must be applied tightly enough to prevent them slipping and becoming unfastened – which can be dangerous when a horse is working – but not so tight that they cause undue pressure on the tendons or restrict the circulation. They must be applied with even pressure and are best secured with needle and thread. Tape may be used but care must be taken that it is

1 Before applying exercise bandages, first wrap the leg in a layer of Gamgee tissue or other suitable padding.

2 Start bandaging at the top, leaving a flap loose as shown. Exercise bandages are made of stretch material.

3 Turn down the flap and bandage over it, overlapping two-thirds of the width of the bandage at each turn.

4 Always apply nearside leg bandages in an anti-clockwise direction and offside ones in a clockwise direction.

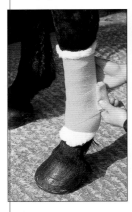

5 Bandage down to the fetlock joint and up again, keeping an even pressure at each turn.

6 Fasten the tapes on the outside of the leg – never at the back or the front.

7 Tie (or sew) the tapes securely, making sure that they are no tighter than the bandage.

8 For neatness and safety, tuck away any loose ends of tape. Exercise bandages should be firm but not overtight.

1 Stable bandages are wider than exercise bandages and are fitted over longer pieces of Gamgee for warmth.

2 The bandage is put on less firmly than an exercise bandage. There must be no wrinkles.

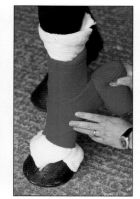

3 Bandage right down to the coronet, overlapping half the width at each turn.

4 Finish the bandage at the top, just below the knee or hock.

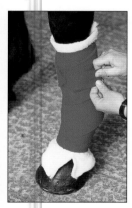

5 Velcro is a quick and convenient method of fastening stable bandages.

■ RIGHT
Sewing the tapes of a bandage in place is the most secure way of finishing off.

■ RIGHT
As an alternative to tieing or sewing the tapes, strong adhesive tape may be used to hold the bandages in place.

When a horse has a leg injury it is usual to bandage the opposite leg with a support bandage (that is an exercise-type bandage) since the horse will be putting more weight and so more strain on this leg while the injury repairs.

SAFETY CHECKLIST

☞ Ensure that the legs are free of dirt and sweat before applying bandages to protect them from being rubbed sore.

☞ Keep bandages clean – avoid washing them in biological powders as some horses are sensitive to them.

☞ Apply bandages over a layer of Gamgee or other padding.

☞ Apply bandages with even pressure.

☞ Apply bandages in an anti-clockwise direction on the nearside legs and clockwise on the offside.

☞ Sew or tape exercise bandages in place with the same pressure as the bandage.

☞ Do not fit exercise bandages too low – they will interfere with the horse's movement and will tend to slip down.

☞ Always tie tapes, when used, on the outside of the legs, never on the inside or at the back or front.

☞ Never apply a bandage to one leg without also bandaging its opposite number.

☞ Remove and replace stable bandages at regular intervals.

not applied tighter than the bandage itself, otherwise it will cause pressure on the tendons.

Exercise bandages should be fitted low enough to afford protection to the sesamoid bones at the rear of the fetlock but not so low that they restrict the movement of the fetlock joint.

For competition purposes self-adhesive bandages are often used nowadays. These tend to exert more pressure than the non-adhesive variety so great care is required when fitting them.

Stable bandages are designed to keep a horse's legs warm, particularly

if he has had a full clip. The bandages are usually about 4½ inches (11cm) wide and are traditionally made of wool although nowadays they are also available in several other materials, including the thermal variety. They should be fitted over a layer of Gamgee or similar padding and must not be applied too tightly, otherwise they will restrict the circulation. The tape fastenings should always be tied on the outside, never on the back of the tendon and care must be taken not to make them too tight. To ensure the horse's comfort, stable bandages should be removed and reapplied at least twice daily.

Boots

Boots of various types may be fitted to protect the horse's legs from injury during exercise and competition. Some horses are apt to knock one leg with another during work because of a conformational irregularity. Young horses are especially vulnerable to injury because they are less well balanced when being ridden than older, more experienced ones; also tired horses, for example those nearing the end of a cross-country course, may become less well co-ordinated. Ground conditions will also affect the horse's legs, hard going making it more likely that the horse will jar himself and deep, muddy going making overreaches more likely.

Boots may be made of leather, with strap fastenings, or from synthetic materials such as PVC and Neoprene, which are easier to clean. These usually have quick-adjusting Velcro or clip fastenings.

Knee boots, consisting of a padded leather kneecap, should be fitted when exercising on the road where it is all too easy for a horse to slip up. The top, elasticated strap should be fastened just tight enough to keep the boot in place, the lower one should be loose so as not to impede the horse's action.

Brushing boots may be fitted on the forelegs and/or hindlegs to prevent injury caused by one leg knocking against the other. This is known as "brushing". Brushing usually occurs on or in the region of the fetlock joint. If the horse knocks his own legs higher up, for example just under the hock, it is known as "speedy cutting".

Overreach boots are fitted to prevent injury to the heels of the forelegs from the toes of the hindlegs. They are bell-shaped and usually made of strong rubber or Neoprene. Those made with "petals" (overlapping sections) give the best protection as they do not invert during use. Boots which are fitted with a strap are much easier to put on and take off than the old type of pull-on boots.

Open-fronted leather tendon boots protect the tendons from being struck by the toes of the hindfeet – a potentially dangerous injury.

Kneeboots are a wise precaution when exercising on the road. The type of boot illustrated is known as a skeleton kneeboot.

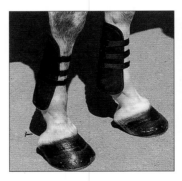

Many modern boots are fitted with quick-release clips or Velcro which are easier to put on and take off than traditional buckles and straps.

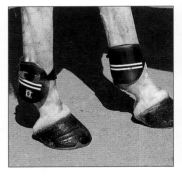

Fetlock boots protect the joints from injury caused by brushing – that is the horse hitting one leg with its opposite number. They come in varying depths.

Tendon boots give a limited amount of support to the tendons and protect them from injury. They are used as an alternative to bandages for fast work and jumping. They come in a variety of designs and materials for both fore and hindlegs.

▌ LEFT
Petal-type overreach boots are easy to fit and do not invert in use. Damaged "petals" can be replaced. They protect the heels of the forelegs.

Travelling Equipment

The horse should always wear
protective clothing when travelling.
His most vulnerable parts are his legs,
particularly the coronets – which he
might easily strike into with his other
feet if he is suddenly thrown off balance
– and his poll. To guard against injury
if he throws his head up he should
wear a poll guard – a piece of padded
leather which is fitted to his headcollar.

Specially designed travelling boots
give protection to the horse's entire
lower legs, including the knees, hocks
and coronets. They usually fasten with
Velcro and are quick and easy to put
on and take off. Alternatively the legs
can be protected with travelling
bandages applied over suitable
padding, such as Gamgee. The
Gamgee should cover the coronets
and the bandages be applied evenly
and not too tightly. Overreach boots

may be fitted and kneeboots should
also be used.

Hock boots will protect a horse
who is inclined to kick during
travelling. The horse may object to
hock boots the first time he wears
them so they should be fitted a few
times in the stable first until he
becomes accustomed to them.

To prevent his tail becoming

rubbed he should wear a tail bandage
and tail guard. The latter fastens
round the tail (over the bandage) and
is attached to the roller of the rug.
Depending on the weather, the horse
should wear a sheet or rug. He should
be kept warm but not be allowed to
become sweaty. Frequent checks
should be made during travelling to
ensure that he is neither too hot nor
too cold.

The horse should be travelled in a
leather headcollar with a lead rope,
preferably one that is attached with a
quick-release mechanism in case of
emergencies. You will have more
control over the horse if you slip a
snaffle bridle (without a noseband)
over the headcollar during loading
and unloading and lead him on the
reins and the headcollar rope rather
than just on the rope.

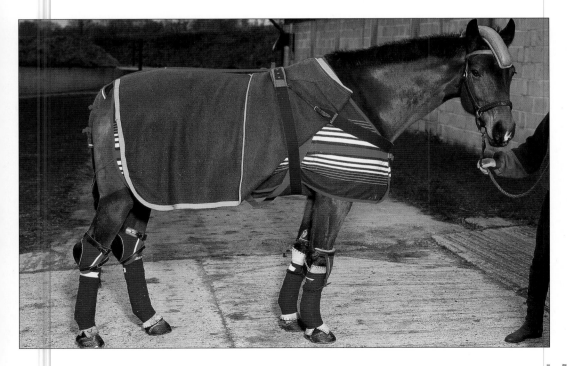

Clothes

When working with horses, whether you are on the ground or riding, safety is the keynote. Horses are big, strong animals and there is always an element of danger, however calm and placid they might normally be. Therefore care should be taken even when choosing clothes for mundane, everyday chores such as mucking out.

Neat clothing which is well fitting without being too tight is the easiest to move around in. A long-sleeved shirt with a sweatshirt or sweater, depending on the weather, and a pair of comfortable trousers, jeans or jodhpurs are ideal for stable work. Avoid overtight trousers as they make bending down difficult. Dark colours will stay looking smart longer. Long sleeves are preferable to short ones since they give some protection from nips from equine teeth. Sleeveless suntops and vests should definitely be avoided.

Footwear is of great importance since a misplaced hoof can do a great deal of damage to a human foot. "Trainers" give little protection, so do most rubber boots, though sturdy Wellingtons are as good as anything for mucking out, particularly if you wear thick walking-boot socks inside. At other times a pair of leather jodhpur boots will probably afford the best protection and will certainly enable you to move more quickly than when wearing Wellingtons. Some boots are now fitted with protective toecaps.

Coats and body warmers, when worn, should be kept fastened – a flapping coat can frighten a nervous horse and there is also the danger that it might become caught up on some "foreign body". Some horses are nervous of noisy waterproof fabrics, so avoid wearing them around the stables.

Long hair should be tied up, again to avoid the possibility of scaring a horse or becoming caught up. This is particularly important in windy weather. Avoid wearing jewellery: rings, earrings, noserings and the like

can all cause nasty injuries if they become caught up.

Most well-trained horses are safe to lead about, in and out of their stables, down to the paddock, etc. But if you have any doubts whatsoever about a horse's good behaviour (when handling a young horse, for example) take precautions: wear a hard hat, correctly fastened, in case he rears up and strikes out, boots to protect your feet and a pair of gloves.

■ ABOVE
A sweatshirt, breeches, boots and a hard hat make a suitable outfit for everyday exercise.

■ LEFT
Neat, workmanlike clothes enable you to carry out daily chores in comfort and safety.

Safety Gear

Riding has always been and always will be a risk sport. But modern safety equipment is constantly improving and everyone who rides should ensure that they wear the best available protective gear, which includes hat, body protector and boots.

The most vulnerable part of the rider is the head and it is irresponsible to get on to a horse, or to lunge or long rein or otherwise handle an

■ LEFT
Fluorescent clothing is a wise safety precaution when riding on the roads. The message on the tabard helps to alert drivers.

SAFETY CHECKLIST

- ✒ Wear a correctly fitting hard hat with the chin strap fastened at all times when mounted.
- ✒ Replace a hat that has been subjected to impact in a fall – it may not give sufficient protection next time.
- ✒ Always ride in your own hat – a borrowed hat is unlikely to fit you correctly.
- ✒ Wear safe footwear at all times when mounted.
- ✒ Always use the correct stirrup iron size – about 1 inch (2.5cm) wider than your boot – to prevent your foot becoming stuck.
- ✒ Wear fluorescent garments – hat cover, tabard/body warmer etc – fitted with retro-reflective strips when riding on the roads and fit your horse with similar high visibility leg bands.
- ✒ Avoid riding on the roads in poor visibility and after dark.
- ✒ Never ride in jewellery.
- ✒ Always fasten tiepins horizontally or at an angle, never vertically.
- ✒ Always ride with your coat fastened.
- ✒ Never take off a coat or sweater while mounted – while you are taking your arms out of the sleeves you will have no control over the horse should he make an unexpected move.
- ✒ If you have less than perfect eyesight, wear soft contact lenses if possible. If not, seek your optician's advice on the safest type of spectacles.

unpredictable young horse, without wearing a **hard hat** securely fastened with a **chin strap**. Your country's national federation (for example in Britain the British Horse Society, in the United States the American Horse Shows Association) will advise on the most up-to-date safety standards. The **jockey skull**, or **crash hat**, is generally considered to give maximum protection and is therefore recommended (and obligatory under the rules of most sports) for all riding which involves fast work or jumping. The **chin harness** must be correctly adjusted and fastened at all times. It may be worn on the point of the chin, with a chin cup, or under the chin, whichever is most comfortable. The alternative is the traditional **hunting cap** which must have a soft peak (a hard peak can cause facial, head or neck injuries in a fall). All riding hats

should be correctly fitted (many retailers are trained in hat fitting).

Body protectors are designed to protect the torso and the shoulders in the event of a fall. They should fit well, feel comfortable and not restrict the rider's movement.

Riding boots and **jodhpur boots** are designed to prevent the foot from sliding right through the stirrup iron or otherwise becoming caught up in the iron in the event of a fall – a potentially fatal situation. They have smooth soles and a clearly defined heel. Leather boots afford the best protection from knocks, for example when riding across country, but rubber ones fashioned in the same style are suitable for everyday riding. Wellington boots, trainers and other boots or shoes with ridged soles and little or no heel should never be worn for riding.

■ LEFT
A jockey skull or "crash hat", with a correctly adjusted chin harness, gives the head maximum protection. It is fitted with a silk cover.

■ LEFT
A body protector should be worn when jumping fixed fences and by people needing special protection (for example, an older person with more brittle bones).

Riding Clothes

By and large all riding clothes are designed for comfort and protection. Only with the odd item of equipment (such as the top hat for dressage) is clothing dictated by fashion.

Most riding clothes are based on hunting attire, which evolved over a long period and led to the design of an entire outfit which would give protection from wet, cold and the many knocks experienced when travelling at speed across country. Long leather boots keep the feet and lower legs dry and give maximum protection from painful encounters with gateposts or other fixed objects. Breeches keep the upper legs warm and dry and protect the insides of the knees from chafing against the saddle. A well-fitting jacket made of a good stout tweed or twill gives warmth and a certain amount of waterproofing while at the same time affording complete freedom of movement – essential for all riding, but particularly for jumping and riding at speed. Gloves keep the hands warm and dry and give a secure grip on the reins. A hunting tie or stock helps protect the neck in the event of a fall. A hard hat, correctly secured with a chin harness, protects the most vulnerable part of all, the head.

For everyday riding there is a wealth of suitable clothing to choose from which is both cheaper than more formal attire and suited to frequent immersion in the washing machine. **Jodhpurs**, which extend down the leg to the ankle, and are usually worn with short, elastic-sided leather jodhpur boots, are cooler in summer than breeches and long boots. They come in a range of materials, from lightweight cotton suitable for hot climates to thermal material for wear in extremes of cold. Instead of jodhpur boots, jodhpurs may be worn with **half-chaps**, which cover the leg from below the knee to the foot, or with full **chaps**, which extend up to the thigh.

Close-fitting **riding trousers** are also suitable for everyday wear. Like

▮ LEFT
Everyday riding clothes should be neat and safe. Dark colours are more practical than the light shades worn with traditional hunting dress.

▮ BELOW LEFT
Chaps are a good alternative to boots. This rider is prepared for roadwork – note the fluorescent tabard and the horse's protective boots.

jodhpurs, they come with "strappings" – reinforcements at the knee and thigh. Some garments are also fitted with an inset seat panel made in an extra-grip material.

Rubber **riding boots** are a cheaper alternative to leather ones, though they can be cold in winter, when an

inner sole or an extra pair of socks may be required.

Casual **riding coats** such as waxed or quilted jackets, blousons and body warmers are fine for everyday riding and may be worn with a shirt and/or sweatshirt or sweater. Modern waterproof materials are light and comfortable to wear and the more expensive ones have the advantage of being "breathable". Waterproofs come in a range of lengths and may have added features such as storm collar and cuffs, fleecy lining and pommel flap. Noisy waterproof materials should be avoided as horses tend to be frightened of them, particularly on a windy day.

There are **gloves** for every occasion, specially designed for the rider. Special features include reinforced rein fingers, pimple palm grips and lycra inserts for extra flexibility.

Clothes for Competition

For most forms of competitive riding it is usual to wear a riding coat with breeches and boots, a shirt with a collar and tie or collarless shirt with a hunting tie or stock. The rules of some sports also stipulate the wearing of spurs. A hat is obligatory and although the bowler hat (derby) is still seen in show classes and the top hat in dressage, the trend is more and more to the safer type of hunting cap and, even more so, the jockey skull. The latter is usually worn with a dark-coloured silk cover.

For cross-country riding the jacket is replaced by a sweater or shirt, according to the weather, which may be in the rider's own colours, as may the hat silk.

Endurance riding is one area where tradition holds less sway, partly because the sport is of fairly recent origin (at least in an organized competitive way) and also because at the higher echelons riders are not only in the saddle for very long periods but also spend some of the time on their feet, running alongside their horses to give them a breather. Breeches and boots would be too hot and uncomfortable so this is the one sport where runningshoes are permitted. However, as a safety precaution, riders are required to use enclosed-type stirrup irons to prevent their feet slipping right through.

▌ LEFT
Correct dress for top-level dressage includes a top hat, tail coat and waistcoat.

▌ BELOW
Most riding gear, for women as well as men, is based on clothes developed for the hunting field.

▌ BOTTOM LEFT
The clothes worn for endurance riding are less formal than in other competitive sports.

Grooming

Regular grooming is an essential part of good horse management. It is not simply a question of making the horse look smart. Far more important is the fact that thorough brushing helps keep the horse healthy by removing accumulated dust, dead skin and hair and helping to keep the pores open and clean. During hard work the horse's skin excretes waste matter in the form of sweat. It is important that the skin and coat are kept clean to enable this system to work efficiently. A good, strenuous grooming also serves as a massage, improving the horse's muscle tone. In addition, grooming helps to keep the horse's tack and rugs clean, which in turn prevents sores. While the stabled horse needs daily grooming both before and after exercise, the grass-kept horse requires far less attention. Although the areas under the saddle and bridle must always be cleaned before tacking up, only the worst of the mud or grease should be removed elsewhere for appearances' sake. Horses and ponies who live out need the natural grease and dirt in their coats to help keep them warm and dry. This is particularly important in winter.

Grooming Kit

The **dandy brush** has long, stiff bristles and is used for removing dried mud and stable stains (where the horse has lain in its droppings or wet bedding) from the legs. It is too harsh to use on the horse's body or on the mane and tail.

The **body brush** has shorter, finer bristles than the dandy brush and may be used on the horse's entire body (and legs). It has a loop for the hand (leather or canvas are the most comfortable). The best body brushes have a leather back which is less likely than wood or plastic to hurt the horse if you inadvertently knock him with it while grooming. Leather, being softer and flexible, also sits more comfortably on the hand.

The body brush is cleaned after every few strokes by drawing the bristles across the teeth of the **metal curry comb**. The metal curry comb should never be used on the horse.

For dampening down the mane and tail the **water brush** is used. This usually has a wooden back and has softer bristles than the dandy brush.

Two **sponges** are required, one for cleaning the eyes and nostrils, the other for use on the dock and the gelding's sheath. The sponges should never be interchanged (having two different colours prevents them being muddled up). They should be washed out after each use.

The **hoof pick** is a vital piece of equipment, used for cleaning out the horse's feet. The end of the pick should be blunt to prevent damage to the foot. Hoof picks are easily dropped and lost in the bedding. It is a good idea to tie a piece of brightly coloured twine to the handle to make it easier to locate.

▌ **RIGHT**
The grooming kit should include trimming scissors, thinning scissors and mane combs for use when trimming the heels, and when pulling the mane and tail.

▌ **PREVIOUS PAGE OPPOSITE**
Quarter marks put the finishing touch to a show pony.

▌ **PREVIOUS PAGE**
Grey horses, like this Percheron, take more keeping clean than dark-coloured horses.

▌ **CLOCKWISE FROM LEFT**
Body brush and metal curry comb; dandy brush; water brush; rubber and plastic curry combs; 'cactus' cloth.

A **stable rubber**, usually made of cloth, is used, slightly dampened, to give a final polish to the horse's coat. A piece of chamois leather or jute sacking is equally effective for this purpose.

A **rubber** or **plastic curry comb**, which like the body brush is fitted with a loop for the hand, may be used for removing dried mud from the coat. Care must be taken when using it on bony areas such as the legs.

A **sweat scraper** is used to remove excess water from the horse's coat after washing him down. It consists of a blade of rubber attached to a metal frame with a handle. Again care must be taken not to knock the bony parts of his body.

Also in the grooming kit will be a **metal mane comb** which is not actually required for the grooming process but for use during trimming the mane and tail. The mane comb may have thick, widely spaced teeth or thin, closer ones.

All grooming tools should be kept tidily in a container designed for the

purpose. Brushes should normally be kept bristle-side up (the bristles will last longer that way). They should be kept clean by regular washing. Since hot water may soften the glue which holds bristles in place, the whole brush should be plunged into cold water after cleaning and stood bristle-side down while it dries (this is particularly important for wooden-backed brushes as the wood will

deteriorate if it is left wet for long periods). All other items of grooming equipment should also be kept scrupulously clean.

For **wisping** – a form of massage involving a rhythmic thumping of the muscles of the neck, shoulders and quarters – a pad is required. Traditionally wisping was carried out with a hay wisp, made by twisting a rope of hay into a firm pad. Nowadays special pads are obtainable, often made of leather.

Sometimes the horse may need to have his mane and tail washed and occasionally his whole body. Buckets, sponges, an appropriate horse shampoo (if necessary), sweat scraper and towels will be required.

Electric groomers, which operate like a household vacuum cleaner, are useful for removing grease and dirt particularly from a horse who has not been clipped. Because of the noise horses must be introduced to them carefully and the tail should always be plaited up out of the way to avoid the possibility of the hair becoming caught up if the groomer has a rotating brush. An electric groomer is not suitable for use on the horse's head. While electric groomers are useful for removing dust and dirt, they do not provide the same massaging effect as a good hand grooming.

▌ RIGHT
A good hoof pick is an essential item of equipment. The one on the left is fitted with a brush which is used after the pick to remove remnants of dirt from the feet.

Grooming Technique

The stabled horse needs a thorough grooming every day. This is best carried out after exercise when the horse is warm. The pores of the skin will be open and grease and dirt will be easier to remove. The horse should be tied up during grooming.

Each **foot** should be picked up and carefully cleaned out with the hoof pick. The pick should be used from the horse's heel towards the toe to avoid damaging the frog. Dirt from the feet should be placed in a skip, not in the horse's bed.

The body brush is used to clean the horse's entire **body,** starting with the neck and working down to the shoulders and the front legs, along the body, over the hindquarters and down the hindlegs. Use the brush – in the left hand for the nearside, in the right hand for the offside – with brisk,

firm strokes and after every few strokes clean the bristles on the metal curry comb, which is held in the other hand. Periodically the dirt should be tapped from the curry comb. This should be done in the doorway or just outside the stable, not into the bedding. Care should be taken when grooming not to bang the horse's bony projections, for example those of the hips and legs, and the brush should not be used with too much pressure over the loins. Having completed one side,

move round to the other side of the horse and repeat the process.

The body brush is also used to clean the **head,** which should be done very gently. The horse should not be tied up for this, in case he pulls back. The headcollar should be fastened round his neck, leaving his nose free.

Brush out the **mane** and **tail** with the body brush, taking care not to break the hairs. The tail should be held away from the horse's body with your free hand and brushed out a

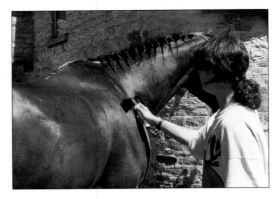

■ LEFT
A very sweaty or dirty horse may be washed down provided he can be dried quickly to prevent chilling. Excess water is removed with a sweat scraper.

1 Grooming begins with picking out the feet. The hoof pick shold always be used from the heel towards the toe.

2 Remnants of dirt may be removed from the area round the frog with a brush.

3 The hoof wall should be kept clean – a stiff brush may be used to remove mud and other forms of dirt.

1 The body brush is used to give the entire body a thorough grooming. It should be used in the direction of the lie of the coat.

2 The curry comb is held in the spare hand and used for cleaning the body brush – never use it on the horse.

3 The dock should be sponged each time the horse is groomed. Use a different sponge from the one used for the eyes and nose.

1 Tail bandages are made of elasticated cotton and are about 3 inches (8cm) wide and 10 feet (3m) long.

2 The bandage is started high up, as near as possible to the top of the dock.

3 A loose flap is left at the top and then turned down and bandaged over. This helps prevent slipping.

4 The bandage is applied down the length of the dock and up again. It should not be fitted too tightly.

5 The bandage is secured with tapes and the dock should be eased into its natural shape.

lock at a time. Any tangles should be teased out with the fingers. A very muddy tail will need washing. To finish off the mane and tail, dip the bristles of the water brush in clean water (not the horse's drinking water) and go lightly over the mane to "lay" it down smoothly. Do the same to the top hairs of the tail. A pulled tail should be bandaged for an hour or so afterwards to keep it tidy.

Use a damp sponge to clean the horse's **eyes** and **nostrils** and another for the **dock.** In the case of geldings the **sheath** will need sponging out once every couple of weeks or so to remove the greasy discharge which accumulates and can cause the horse discomfort. Special solutions can be obtained for this purpose or you can use a mild soap and warm water. Use the same sponge that is used for cleaning his dock. The easiest time to give him a thorough clean in this area is when he is staling. Do it carefully and gently – and beware of being kicked should the horse object. If you are unable to catch the moment when the horse is staling, clean out the sheath by gently inserting the sponge inside it and cleaning all round. Rinse the whole area several times and dry off with a towel.

The finishing touch to the whole grooming process is applied by running a damp stable rubber or other cloth over the entire coat to add a final polish. Wisping with a hay wisp or pad, when done, takes place after regular grooming since its purpose is not to clean but to **massage.** The pad or wisp is applied in much the same

GROOMING TIPS

☞ Never try to groom a sweaty horse – walk him about until he is dry.

☞ Never try to brush off wet mud – either hose it off or let it dry first.

☞ To dry off a wet horse in the stable cover him with a sheet or rug made of "breathable" material or put a layer of straw along his back and quarters with a rug over the top (this is known as "thatching").

☞ To remove dried mud use a dandy brush or rubber curry comb but not too roughly – it may be necessary to remove mud from sensitive areas of skin, such as inside the hindlegs, with your hand.

☞ In cold weather keep a clipped horse warm during grooming by turning his rugs back and forward (as when quartering) rather than removing them altogether.

☞ Give all rugs and blankets a thorough shaking every week – it is pointless to put dusty rugs back on to a clean horse.

☞ Never stand directly behind a horse.

☞ Never sit or kneel on the floor to reach the lower parts – always squat or bend so that you can move quickly if he does.

☞ Keep a watchful eye open for any skin injuries or tell-tail lumps or bumps, particularly on the legs, which could warn of impending soundness problems.

☞ With the grass-kept horse clean the area under the saddle and brush off the worst of the mud for appearances' sake but do not attempt regular, thorough grooming.

way as a brush, but with a firmer thump (though not too hard). It is used on the large muscular areas of the horse (the neck, shoulders and quarters). It is said to improve the circulation and muscle tone. It should never be used on the more tender areas, such as the loins, nor on the bony areas, such as the legs.

A thorough grooming will take from half to three-quarters of an hour, depending on the initial cleanliness of the horse's skin and coat – and the strength and endurance of the groom! Grooming is most effective if you stand a little away from the horse in order to put your weight behind the brush.

A less comprehensive type of grooming called **quartering** is used to prepare the horse in the morning for exercise. Its purpose is to remove any surface dirt accumulated during the night and to make the horse generally presentable. Quartering involves unfastening his rugs, turning them back over his loins and giving his front half a quick brush over, then turning his rugs forward and doing the same to his hind end. Any stains and bedding marks should be removed, if necessary by using a damp sponge or water brush. The damp areas should be dried off with a stable rubber or a towel. The mane and tail should be brushed through and all traces of bedding removed. The feet should be picked clean and the eyes, nostrils and dock sponged. Quartering takes between ten and twenty minutes, depending on the horse's size and how dirty he is.

Types of Clip

In winter horses grow a thick coat to protect them from the weather. A horse with a thick coat who is required to do anything other than light work will sweat excessively and, as a result, be very uncomfortable, lose condition and run the risk of catching a chill if he is not carefully dried off after exercise. Clipping off the thick winter coat of the stabled horse removes these problems and also makes it easier to keep the horse clean and looking smart. A clipped horse must be kept warm with blankets and rugs. A clipped horse who spends some time out at grass will need a waterproof New Zealand rug.

There are different ways of clipping a horse or pony, depending on the work he is required to do and the type of coat he grows. A **full clip** involves removing the coat from the entire body and the legs. A thick-coated horse may be given a full clip when he is first clipped and then at subsequent clippings have his legs left unclipped. Leaving the hair on the legs affords some protection from knocks. The

full clip is usually only used for horses in very fast work, such as racing, or sometimes for a show horse being prepared for early spring shows.

The most usual clip for other horses doing hard work is the **hunter clip** which involves leaving the hair on the legs and the area under the saddle. Again the reason for leaving legs and saddle patch unclipped is to provide protection. Care must be taken to dry off the saddle patch thoroughly after work.

As its name suggests the **blanket clip** involves leaving an area of the horse's back, loins and quarters unclipped (and also the legs). The hair is removed from the neck, shoulders and belly and all or part of the head. A blanket clip is suitable for a horse doing a fair amount of medium to hard work.

Horses who are kept out, and stabled horses not in hard work, may be given a low **trace clip,** which consists of removing the hair from the underside of the neck, between the forelegs, the belly and the upper

part of the hind legs. Medium and high trace clips, which involve removing more of the body and neck hair are suitable for stabled horses in steady work.

With the **chaser clip** the hair is removed from the head, the lower part of the neck, the chest, the belly and the upper part of the hindlegs. The clip finishes just behind the ears. It is often used on steeplechasers (hence its name). Many Thoroughbred horses have fine coats which may not require total removal even when they are in hard work.

There are various other partial clips suitable for the grass-kept horse used only for light work such as occasional hacking. These include the **bib clip** and the **apron clip.** In the bib clip the coat is removed only from the jowl, down the underside of the neck down to and including the front of the chest. In the apron clip an area above the forelegs and extending back under the girth area of the body is also removed. These areas, together with the flanks and the inside of the hindlegs, are usually the first to become sweaty. A tough animal, such as a native pony, could probably live out without rugs after having a bib or apron clip though in very adverse weather he might need to be rugged. When clipping the hair from the hindquarters an inverted V is left at the top of the tail. The unclipped leg hair is sloped at the top from front to back.

The horse's head is a particularly vulnerable spot because of its thin covering of skin and hair. Many people leave the head unclipped or simply clip the lower half which effectively removes the hair from the sweatiest part (i.e. the jowl) while leaving the top half with protection from the weather. Many horses dislike having their heads clipped at all. This can be caused by a number of reasons, from fear of the sound or feel of the clippers to painful conditions such as toothache or an ear infection.

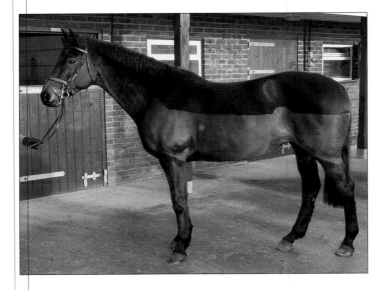

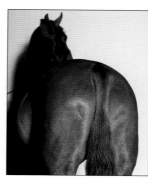

▮ ABOVE
This horse has been blanket clipped. The clipping lines should be carefully marked on the horse beforehand, using chalk or a damp bar of saddle soap.

▮ ABOVE RIGHT
The area above the tail is finished off in a neat V shape. Care must be taken not to cut into either the mane or tail hair.

▮ LEFT
The Irish clip involves removing the hair from the belly and chest and part of the shoulders and neck. This horse has had his head clipped, too.

▮ OPPOSITE PAGE
A trace clip is suitable for stabled horses not in hard work. The body and neck may be clipped higher or lower depending on the amount of work the horse is doing.

▮ LEFT
For the horse in hard work the hunter clip is most suitable. A full or part saddle patch (as here) should be left to protect the back.

Clipping and Trimming

Clipping horses is hard work and can be dangerous. It should never be carried out alone. The beginner should learn the techniques by watching an expert at work. If in doubt, find someone else to clip your horse, at least to begin with so that you can find out how he behaves.

Having decided on the type of clip, all lines (for example the leg lines and saddle patch) should be marked on the horse's coat with chalk or a damp piece of saddle soap. To mark the saddle patch put the horse's usual saddle on his back, without its fittings, make sure it is in the position where it lies when he is being ridden, and draw round it. It is better to make the saddle patch a little larger than it will finally need to be to make allowance for any mistakes when clipping the edges. A badly positioned saddle patch will spoil the look of the horse.

Start clipping at the front of the horse, on the neck or shoulder, and work your way backwards section by section. The clippers should be used against the lie of the coat (broadly speaking from the back of the horse towards the front) with long, sweeping strokes. Each stroke should be parallel to the one above or below it and should slightly overlap the previous one.

Take care when clipping the top line of the neck not to cut into the mane. Clip a short bridle path out of the mane just behind the ears where

■ RIGHT
Essential clipping and trimming equipment: electric clippers, electric and battery driven trimmers, spare clipper blades, oil, small brush (for cleaning clogged blades) and screwdriver (for changing fuses if necessary).

the headpiece of the bridle lies. This does not need to be very long: 2 inches (5cm) is adequate.

After the neck and shoulders clip the body and finally the hindquarters. Be particularly careful when clipping awkward places such as the delicate skin below the stifle and the folds between the front legs. The stifle skin should be held with your spare hand to straighten out the folds. An assistant should hold each foreleg up and forward in turn to stretch the folds of skin. Holding up a foreleg will also help prevent a horse from fidgeting or kicking. When clipping between the hindlegs be particularly watchful in case the horse does try to kick out. Keeping hold of his tail will help to prevent this.

The most difficult part of the horse to clip well is the head. If a horse is really frightened of having the clippers near his head it is far better

to leave it unclipped. If the horse's head is to be clipped, first remove the headcollar. If he will not stand still without some form of restraint a halter is easier to work round with the clippers than a headcollar. Where you start will depend very much on the horse but the cheeks are probably the best place. Rest the clippers, switched off, against the cheekbone for a few moments until the horse becomes used to their presence. Then if he does not object switch on and work carefully over both cheeks, underneath from the chin to the throat, up over the front of the head and over the forehead. Because the head is so bony the clippers should be used as lightly as possible to reduce vibration. Be particularly careful when working near the eye.

Some people clip off the horse's whiskers round his muzzle but since

The mane is shortened and thinned by means of pulling, using a mane comb. Remove only a few hairs at a time to prevent soreness and damp the mane down afterwards.

To neaten an untidy tail, pull hair from the sides and centre of the dock, preferably when the horse is warm and the pores are open.

A mane comb and sharp, round-ended scissors are used to trim excess hair from the pasterns and fetlocks of unclipped legs. Take care not to leave "steps" of hair.

■ RIGHT
Holding up a foreleg
smooths out skin
creases and also
stops the horse
fidgeting.

**■ MIDDLE
RIGHT**
Proceed carefully
and gently when
clipping the head.

**■ BOTTOM
RIGHT**
Holding the tail
helps prevent a
horse from kicking.
The tail is bandaged
to keep it clear of
the clipper blades.

CLIPPING AND TRIMMING TIPS

☛ During clipping feel the underside of the blades every few minutes – if they are becoming hot, switch off and allow them to cool down before continuing.

☛ During clipping clean and oil the blades every ten to fifteen minutes.

☛ During clipping keep the horse warm by throwing a rug over the clipped areas – a cold horse will fidget more than a warm one.

☛ Always clip in good light conditions – start in the morning.

☛ Never try to clip a sweaty or dirty horse.

☛ For the best results do not clip until the horse's winter coat has "set" (i.e. is fully grown) – usually mid-autumn.

☛ To gauge the correct position and angle of leg lines measure one hand's width from where the foreleg joins the chest (for the V) and two hands' widths below the elbow; measure four hands' widths below the top of the stifle on the hindleg and two hands' widths above the point of the hock.

☛ Accustom a nervous horse to the feel of clippers by running hand clippers (i.e. non-motorized ones) over him.

☛ Have clippers serviced, and the blades reground, regularly.

☛ Ask your veterinary surgeon to administer a sedative to a horse who is really dangerous to clip.

☛ Pull manes and tails when the horse is warm, either on a hot day or after exercise – the hair will come out more easily while the pores are open, which is easier for you and more comfortable for the horse.

☛ Pull hair, whenever possible, from the underside of the mane – this will encourage it to lie flat.

these are used as sensors it is preferable, and kinder, to leave them alone.

To trim the ears, hold each one in turn and run the clippers along the outside edge only. Never try to clip the hair from inside the ear as the horse needs this as protection from insects and dirt. Never clip the eyelashes. Be careful when clipping the top of the head not to cut into the forelock.

If the horse's legs are left unclipped it will probably be necessary to trim his fetlocks and pasterns to make him look tidy. Use a mane comb and scissors (with rounded ends for safety) to remove excess feather, taking care not to create "steps" of hair but to leave a smooth line. Trim any thick hair from around the coronet.

If the horse's head is left unclipped, long hairs around the jaw may also be removed with scissors and comb. Scissors may be used to trim the long hairs from the edge of the ears.

Manes are kept neat by means of pulling, which involves plucking out strands of hair until the mane is the desired length and thickness. If the horse finds this too uncomfortable, it is possible to tidy up the mane with a thinning comb but never be tempted to use scissors which will give a very unsatisfactory result. Pulling can usually be achieved if you take your time and do only a small section of the mane at a time, spreading the whole job over a number of days.

An untidy tail can also be improved by pulling out some of the hairs from the top of the dock. Hair should be removed from the sides and, to a lesser extent, from the centre. As with

the mane, it is best to remove a few hairs each day to prevent soreness. After pulling, the tail should be dampened with a water brush and bandaged to make the hair lie flat (do not leave the bandage on overnight).

A pulled tail will need regular pulling if it is to keep its neat shape. A horse who lives out during the winter should not have his tail pulled – the hair at the top of the dock is there to protect him from rain and snow. To trim the bottom of the tail, raise the horse's dock to the position where he carries it when he is on the move. With your other hand hold the hair at the bottom of the tail and then cut off the hair to the required length. The end of the tail should be parallel to the ground when the horse is moving.

Final Touches for Turnout

Plaiting, or **braiding, the mane** makes the horse or pony look smart, particularly if he has an untidy mane and is to appear in public. In some showing classes it is expected that the horse will be plaited. In others, such as those for Mountain and Moorland ponies and Arabs, the mane is never plaited. It is easier to plait a mane that has been pulled – a very thick, uneven mane will result in ugly, untidy plaits.

The mane hair is divided into equal bunches, each of which is dampened and then plaited, turned under and secured close to the crest of the neck, either by sewing with thread or with rubber bands. Sewn plaits are the most secure and are therefore more suitable for the horse engaged in lengthy periods of work such as hunting or eventing. Rubber bands are suitable for sports such as show jumping, where the mane does not need to remain plaited for long.

The plaits need to be fairly tight to look tidy and stay put, but beware of plaiting too tightly. If you do, it can cause the horse discomfort, particularly if he is required to stretch his neck a lot, for example when he is doing fast work or jumping.

A horse's appearance may be greatly improved by clever plaiting: making the plaits in the dip of the neck bigger than the others will help

A plaited forelock gives the head a neat appearance. Plaits should be tight enough to prevent them dropping out but not so tight that they cause the horse discomfort.

Quarter marks add the finishing touches to a well-groomed horse or pony. A chequered pattern may be made with a mane comb and stencil.

disguise a ewe neck; a small number of plaits will make a long neck seem shorter; conversely, a short neck will look longer if the mane has lots of small plaits. The appearance of a horse with a very untidy mane can be improved if the mane is hogged, or clipped off altogether. A hogged mane looks best on a horse of fairly heavy build, such as a cob – in Britain cobs are always shown with a hogged mane. Manes grow quickly and will need re-hogging every few weeks.

Plaiting, or **braiding, a tail** looks complicated but is not too difficult once you have had a little practice. For successful plaiting the tail must have long hair at the top – it is not possible to plait a pulled tail. The hair must be clean, well brushed and dampened before plaiting begins. When the plait is complete it should be carefully dampened with a sponge and then protected with a tail bandage. To avoid damaging the plait the tail bandage must be removed by unwinding, not by sliding it down.

In very muddy conditions, for instance when riding across country in wet weather, it may be more comfortable for the horse to have his tail put up so that it cannot become clogged with mud. To put up a tail, start plaiting from the top in the usual way. When you reach the end of the

1 Plaiting a mane using needle and thread: the end of each plait is secured with thread.

2 The plait is folded or rolled up until it is close to the crest and stitched firmly.

3 Finished plaits should be the same size. Using larger or smaller plaits can help disguise a poorly shaped neck.

1 To plait a tail begin high up, using one bunch of hair from each side and one from the centre.

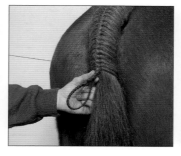

2 Plait down to the end of the dock, using thin bunches of hair from alternate sides.

3 At the end of the dock, stop adding side bunches and continue plaiting the long hair.

dock, divide the rest of the tail into three and continue plaiting to the end of the long tail hairs. The bottom of the plait should be secured with a thick rubber band or needle and thread. The plaited tail is rolled up under the dock and carefully sewn to hold it in place.

For smart occasions, such as showing and racing, the horse's coat may be decorated with **quarter marks.** These are applied on the hindquarters and may be drawn in with a comb, a brush, or by means of brushing over a plastic stencil. All three methods involve producing a pattern by brushing patches of the coat in different directions.

There are various other "tricks of the trade" which will enhance the appearance of a show horse. Chalk may be brushed into white leg markings. It is also useful for disguising any dirty marks on a grey coat, particularly those acquired during travelling, when there is no time to wash and dry the horse before his class. A little baby oil or Vaseline may be rubbed around the eyes and nostrils – this will accentuate the quality of the head. Human hairspray may be used to help control an unruly mane. The horse's coat may be given a final polish with coat gloss, which is specially made for the purpose.

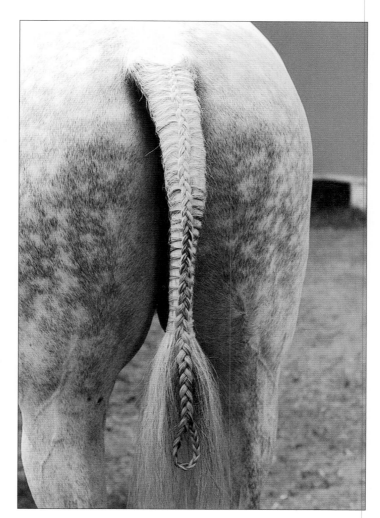

■ RIGHT
The end of the plait is secured with needle and thread, tucked under and sewn in place to give a smart appearance.

Glossary

Bandage Various different bandages are used for the tail, knees and legs for protection, support or warmth as well as to keep wound dressings in place; known in America as leg-wraps.

Brushing Striking the fore or hind leg inside the fetlock joint with the opposite foot while moving.

Cast Term used when a horse, lying down in his stable, becomes wedged in position and can't move or get up.

Chaff Finely chopped hay, sometimes mixed with one-third oat straw. It is added to concentrates to aid digestion.

Compound feeds Concentrates in either cube or coarse mix form. Made from a variety of ingredients to provide a balanced diet.

Concentrates Energy-giving foods such as oats and barley, fed in addition to the bulk feed in varying proportions, depending on the work the horse is required to do.

Conformation The shape and make-up of the horse.

Deep litter bed A bed whereby only the droppings are removed and a fresh layer of bedding laid on top every day.

Dock The part of the spine that runs down the tail.

Fillet string Cord attached to the corners of some rugs, generally made of the same material as the rug, which passes under the tail to help keep the rug in place.

Flexion tests Manipulation of the limbs to detect lameness.

Gamgee tissue Absorbent cotton wool covered with absorbent gauze, used as a padding before the application of bandages to ensure even pressure on the tendons. Invented by Joseph Sampson Gamgee in the nineteenth century.

Gelding Castrated male horse or pony.

Hand Four inches. Horses are over 14.2hh (hands high); ponies are under 14.2hh measured at the withers.

Hack Riding out on roads or cross-country; equivalent of an American trail ride.

Haylage Different nutritional levels of grass, sold in sealed plastic bags. Suitable for horses with respiratory problems.

'Heating' A horse or pony made over-excited possibly by feeding too much concentrate.

Hogged mane A mane that is clipped off altogether. Mainly used for horses of heavy build such as a cob.

Loose box Self-contained indoor stall in which the horse is not tethered.

Lunge To train a horse on a circle from a central position on the ground using a single long lunge rein and long whip.

Manège Enclosure, indoor or outdoor, in which horses are schooled.

Navicular bone Small bone in the horse's foot which articulates with the pedal bone and the pastern.

Salt lick Block of salt fitted into a holder and hung in the horse's stable or on a fence post in the paddock. A salt lick is essential to make up for any salt deficiency in the diet.

School To train a horse.

Skip Bucket-like container made of metal, plastic or rubber for collecting droppings.

Skep See Skip.

Serpentines A series of same-sized half-circles that a horse is required to perform in opposite directions down the length of the manège.

Semi-deep litter system The droppings and the worst of the wet bedding are removed every day and the whole bed mucked out once a week.

Setting fair Tidying the horse's bed for the night, taking care to bank up the sides and making sure the floor is evenly covered.

Stable vices Various unnatural behaviours displayed by horses kept in stables for too long, such as box-walking, crib-biting and weaving, usually the result of boredom.

Surcingle A belt, usually of webbing or elasticated web, that goes round the horse's body. It has various uses but if used to keep a rug in place, it should be passed over a back pad to prevent pressure on the spine. May be passed over the saddle to give extra security. Also known as an over-girth.

Pull a mane/tail Thinning the hairs of the mane and top of the tail by selectively pulling them out.

Roughage Bulk feed such as hay.

Stale To urinate.

Tack Saddlery and other equipment used in the riding and training of horses.

Under/over horsed Riding a horse that is too small/big for you.

▌ OPPOSITE A Cleveland Bay at grass.

Index

Acknowledgements

The author, publisher and
photographer are grateful
to the Catherston Stud,
Whitchurch, Hampshire,
England, and Stretcholt
Farm Stud, Bridgwater,
Somerset for allowing their
horses, ponies and stables
to be photographed.